Intra-Asian
International
Relations

Other Westview Special Studies on China and East Asia

Women in Changing Japan, edited by Joyce Lebra, Joy Paulson, and Elizabeth Powers

Cadres, Commanders, and Commissars: The Training of the Chinese Communist Leadership, 1920-45, Jane L. Price

Mineral Resources and Basic Industries in the People's Republic of China, K. P. Wang

The Problems and Prospects of American–East Asian Relations, edited by John Chay

The Chinese Military System: An Organizational Study of the People's Liberation Army, Harvey Nelsen

The Medieval Chinese Oligarchy, David G. Johnson

Chinese Foreign Policy after the Cultural Revolution, 1966-1977, Robert G. Sutter

The Politics of Medicine in China: The Policy Process, 1949-1977, David M. Lampton

Other Westview Special Studies on South and Southeast Asia

Indira Gandhi's India: A Political System Reappraised, edited by Henry C. Hart

Southeast Asia and China: The End of Containment, Edwin Martin

Westview Special Studies on China and East Asia/South and Southeast Asia

Intra-Asian International Relations
edited by George T. Yu, University of Illinois

This collection of authoritative papers prepared by some of America's most eminent scholars in the field provides us with an up-to-date analysis of the complex and rapidly changing relations among China, Russia, Japan, and the countries of South and Southeast Asia. The contributors discuss in depth the major issues faced by the policymakers of each country, examining also the role of the U.S. in order to furnish greater perspective and a more realistic picture. Among the issues considered are Sino-Soviet relations, interdependence versus national assertiveness, economic interaction, and the effects of international conflict. The analyses of individual countries are supplemented by a broader view of actors and issues in regional and international contexts; equally important, the emphasis on contemporary aspects allows a look at current trends and the dynamics of future Asian international relations.

George T. Yu holds a Ph.D. from the University of California. At present he is professor of political science and Asian studies at the University of Illinois, Urbana.

Intra-Asian
International
Relations

edited by George T. Yu

Westview Press
Boulder, Colorado

Westview Special Studies on China and
East Asia/South and Southeast Asia

Copyright© 1977 by Westview Press
Published in 1977 in the United States of America by
  Westview Press, Inc.
  1898 Flatiron Court
  Boulder, Colorado 80301
  Frederick A. Praeger, Publisher and Editorial Director

Library of Congress Cataloging in Publication Data
Main entry under title:
Intra-Asian international relations.
  (Westview special studies on China and East Asia/South and Southeast Asia)
  "This book originated from a panel organized for the 1976 annual conference of the Association for Asian Studies."
  Bibliography: p.
1. Asia—Politics and government. I. Yu, George T., 1931- II. Association for Asian Studies. III. Series.
DS35.I57   327'.095   77-24382
ISBN 0-89158-125-1

Printed and bound in the United States of America

Contents

The Contributors ix
Preface.. xi

1. Introduction................................ 1
   George T. Yu
2. Intra-Asian Relations: An Overview.............. 9
   Robert A. Scalapino
3. China and the Balance of Power in Asia 31
   A. Doak Barnett
4. The Soviet Union and the Far East 59
   Donald S. Zagoria
5. Japan and Asia: Growing Entanglement 91
   Donald C. Hellmann
6. Southeast Asia Reexamines Its Options 107
   Guy J. Pauker
7. India's Asian Relations 125
   Richard L. Park
8. Asian Actors and Issues....................... 153
   Morton I. Abramowitz

Selected Bibliography 167

The Contributors

Morton I. Abramowitz is a foreign service officer now serving as deputy assistant secretary of defense for international security affairs, Department of Defense. He is the author of *Remaking China Policy* (with Richard Moorsteen) and other works on Asian policies.

A. Doak Barnett, a senior fellow at the Brookings Institution (Washington, D.C.), is the author of *China Policy: Old Problems and New Challenges* and numerous works on contemporary Chinese politics and foreign policy.

Donald C. Hellmann, professor of political science and Asian studies at the University of Washington, Seattle, has written extensively on Japanese politics and the international relations of Asia. Recently he served as editor for two volumes on Asia, *China and Japan: A New Balance of Power* and *Southern Asia: The Politics of Poverty and Peace.*

Richard L. Park is professor of political science at the University of Michigan, Ann Arbor. He has written and edited numerous works on South Asian politics and foreign policies, including *India's Political System* and "India's Foreign Policy," in *Foreign Policy in World Politics* (edited by Roy C. Macridis).

Guy J. Pauker is senior staff member in the Social Science Department of the Rand Corporation. Before 1963 he was chairman of the Center for Southeast Asian Studies at the University of California, Berkeley. His research interests have taken him annually to Southeast Asia for more than two decades.

Robert A. Scalapino is professor of political science and director of the East Asian Center at the University of California, Berkeley. Author of numerous books and articles on Asian politics and Asian and U.S. foreign policies, among his latest publications are *Asia and the Road Ahead: Issues for the Major Powers* and *The Foreign Policy of Modern Japan.*

George T. Yu, professor of political science and Asian studies at the University of Illinios, Urbana-Champaign, has written on Chinese politics and foreign policy. He is the author of *China's African Policy: A Study of Tanzania* and other works.

Donald S. Zagoria is professor of government, Hunter College, New York. He is the author of *The Sino-Soviet Conflict, Vietnam Triangle: Moscow, Peking, Hanoi,* and other works on the politics and foreign policies of Asia.

Preface

This book originated from a panel organized for the 1976 annual conference of the Association for Asian Studies. The five papers presented at the panel by Abramowitz, Barnett, Hellmann, Pauker, and Scalapino have since been revised for inclusion in the present volume. In addition, two papers by Park and Zagoria have been added. I should like to express my appreciation to the contributors for their cooperation. It has been a long struggle, but I know the effort has been worth the labor.

I wish to thank Joyce Kallgren and Mervyn Seldon for their encouragement. My family deserves an extra measure of thanks for their support and patience.

George T. Yu

May 16, 1977
Urbana, Illinois

1. Introduction

George T. Yu

The end of World War II was a watershed in intra-Asian international relations; it brought Western domination of Asia to an end and ushered in a trend toward greater regional autonomy and interaction. To be sure, the Korean War, the Sino-Soviet conflict, the Vietnam War, and other events obscured this new development, exaggerating the continued dependence of Asian countries upon external sources while diverting attention from increasing intra-Asian interaction. The greater level of relations among the regional actors has not meant exclusion of external sources; nor has it meant that Asian countries have severed or intend to sever linkages with countries outside Asia. What developments in Asia have shown has been the changing nature of Asian international relations: toward greater Asianization and more involvement of the Asian states with each other.

This volume is an attempt to analyze the present and future patterns of intra-Asian international relations. There is a great need for such studies of the individual actors, the dominant issues, the patterns of interaction, and the relationships between and among the regional actors and their linkages to the world. For a variety of reasons, our understanding of Asian developments has tended to lag behind the fast pace of events. The post-Vietnam years for Asians and others have been a period of adjustment and uncertainty; they have also been a period of questioning and waiting. This does not excuse specialists on Asia from examining Asian international relations; it does make the work of the specialist exceedingly difficult. A great deal of skill, including an in-depth knowledge of the individual Asian actors and the region *and* training and experience in international political analysis, is required of the specialist for any meaningful assessment of present developments and future trends.

The contributors to this volume have been drawn from among America's most eminent specialists in the field. They know the Asian actors and the region and are skilled analysts of international politics. To the extent practicable, they deal with similar questions and issues; each author has attempted to analyze intra-Asian relations from his special perspective while also considering the impact of his subject upon the larger Asian scene.

One of the fundamental concerns of the contributors has been to examine how the Asian countries perceive their environment and how this perception has influenced their foreign policies and behavior patterns. From their comments on the past and the present, the contributors go on to offer predictions about the future policies and behavior of the Asian countries and intra-Asian relations.

In the first essay, Professor Robert A. Scalapino deals with intra-Asian relations in a broad fashion. After examining some geopolitical factors, the imperial legacies, and the immediate post–World War II era, he looks at the impact of the two events, the two immediate causes, that transformed Asian international relations: the Korean War and the Sino-Soviet conflict. He sees two primary trends. First, there is a trend toward Asianization, including a "more intricate and intensive involvement of the Asian states with each other—in harmony or in conflict." Second, there is a movement away from exclusive linkages toward "the politics of equidistance." Equidistance, according to Professor Scalapino, means for the Asian countries a search "for a position that affords contact with all parties of significance, yet with some

economic, political, or military relations tailored specifically to their particular position."

Professor Scalapino concludes his survey of intra-Asian
relations with an assessment of the future. He sees a trend
toward a balance of weakness, with both internal and
external Asian actors possessing only limited power to
determine developments. Two scenarios are offered; both
promise new directions in intra-Asian international relations.

The centrality of military-security concerns in the foreign
policy and behavior of the People's Republic of China is the
subject of Professor A. Doak Barnett's study of China in Asia.
Professor Barnett argues that major shifts in China's foreign
policy can be best understood in relation to changes in
China's perception of external security threats, especially
when linked to the Sino-Soviet conflict. Three crucial
turning points in the Sino-Soviet conflict are discussed,
points at which vital security considerations were involved
and which are ultimately related to shifts in China's foreign
policy. There follows a discussion of China's overall strategic world view, including comments on the "publicly articulated three-world schema" and the unstated view of the key
roles of the five major power centers. While Professor
Barnett maintains that it is more important to examine what
China actually does, he also recognizes the contribution of
official statements as indications of China's basic approach
to strategic problems. In this context, he examines Mao Tse-
tungs's 1940 directive "On Policy" and the 1971 commentary
written when the directive was republished. Professor
Barnett finds that the documents "are extremely revealing
with regard to strategic premises and assumptions" of
China. Among others, they point to the application of
"flexible united-front strategies."

Looking into the future, Professor Barnett concludes that
security problems will continue to be *the* basic foreign policy
concern of China. However, like Professor Scalapino, he
suggests that China's military weakness or inferiority greatly
limits its pursuit of security, especially against the Soviet

Union or the United States or both.

Professor Donald S. Zagoria explores the important problem of the Soviet Union and Asia. The central question of the essay is why the Soviet Union, despite its massive military power, has been unable to project its power and influence upon Asia. As Professor Zagoria states, the Soviet Union has neither genuine allies nor untroubled relations with the major countries in Asia. To explain this phenomenon, the Soviet Union's relations with China, Japan, and North Korea are examined; the Soviet Union's interaction with southern Asia is also explored. In every instance, the fortunes of the Soviet Union in Asia are found to be at a low ebb.

This is especially true of Soviet relations with China, a major Soviet failure in Asia. A host of factors have contributed to the Sino-Soviet conflict, including cultural, psychological, geopolitical, as well as the factors of national interest and ideology. However, the immediate factor that deepened the conflict was "Soviet overreactions to the Chinese threat," symbolized by the massive Soviet military buildup on the Chinese frontier. Professor Zagoria suggests that it was the Soviet policy of overreaction that "lost" China, "the most significant Russian loss of the entire postwar era."

Professor Zagoria concludes that a primary factor in the low fortunes of the Soviet Union in Asia is "the shortcomings of Moscow's own policy," a policy rigidly concerned with frontier security and massive military buildups. A consequence has been the weak political position of the Soviet Union in Asia.

The success of Japan as a global economic power is well recognized. Less known has been Japan's role in Asia. Professor Donald C. Hellmann explains Japan's growing intra-Asian relations in terms of economic ties, political-diplomatic actions, and Asia as a factor in Japanese domestic politics. These forces, more than Japan's visible global economic role and relations with the major powers, will determine the international future of Japan.

Nowhere does Professor Hellmann better illustrate the all-important Japanese role in Asia than in his discussion of the economic linkages. Comparing Japan's trade since 1970 with the European Economic Community and Hong Kong, South Korea, and Taiwan, he notes that "Tokyo now does almost ninety percent as much trade with two small developing nations and a city-colony in Asia (all resource-poor) as is done with the entire European Economic Community. . . ." Nor is this all. Japan has become the first or second leading trading partner of every country in East and Southeast Asia. Much of Japan's official developmental assistance is concentrated in Asia. In short, a "web of economic intercourse," to use Professor Hellmann's term, has drawn Japan deeply into Asian affairs, making Japan increasingly dependent upon Asia.

Japan's role in Asia has been furthered by a growing political-diplomatic entanglement. This includes deepening relations with the People's Republic of China and a new intensity of contacts with South Korea. Professor Hellmann concludes his essay with a review of Japan's fluid and uncertain domestic political situation, a consequence of changing American policy toward Asia, new Japanese-American relations, and Japan's own internal developments. A problem for the future, given the weakness of Japanese domestic politics in a time of strong foreign policy leadership needs and given Japan's increasing Asian orientation, including mounting dependence upon the "politically volatile and unpredictable developing nations," is Japan's future role in Asia. According to Professor Hellmann, Japan will be taking an uncharted course.

Southeast Asia was once highly visible in global politics. Now, since the end of the Vietnam conflict in 1975, it is of limited interest. But Southeast Asia's own search for a new orientation may be just beginning. Dr. Guy J. Pauker explains the consequences brought on by the end of the war, compares conditions in the region between the present and the 1950s, examines some of the dominant regional political and economic trends, and reviews the relationships between the Southeast Asian countries and the major powers. In every instance, one finds that after the experiences of the Vietnam conflict the countries of Southeast Asia are reassessing their own role and that of the region.

In reviewing the relationships between the countries of Southeast Asia and the major powers, Dr. Pauker suggests a state of great uncertainty. He finds that "none of the major powers seems eager at this time to increase substantially their political and economic involvement in the affairs of Southeast Asia." As for the Southeast Asian countries themselves, the trend seems to be away from dependence upon an external source and toward nonalignment. However, this does not deny the existence of important linkages and the need for such between Southeast Asian countries and states outside the immediate area, as in Japanese–Southeast Asian economic relations. What Dr. Pauker does say is that Southeast Asia is a "high-risk region," with little likelihood in the long run of the development of reliable political alliances or economic partnerships between a Southeast Asian country and a major power.

Dr. Pauker concludes his essay on a somber note. Beset with political and economic tensions on the one hand and with continued importance to the powers due to its strategic location on the other, Southeast Asia will remain a volatile and unpredictable region.

Next, Professor Richard L. Park analyzes India's Asian relations. Beginning with a review of India's domestic and foreign experiences and a survey of its trade patterns, he then examines India's interaction with its Asian neighbors. India's relations with the United States and the Soviet Union are also discussed. As Professor Park notes, India's foreign policy has been most active in South Asia; this has been linked to India's concern with its national security. Directly and indirectly, India's interaction with China, the Soviet Union, and the United States has also been governed by the security issue. Outside of relations with South Asia and the superpowers and China, India's links to Southeast Asia has been moderate, while relations with Japan have been strictly those of trading partners. Professor Park concludes that outside of South Asia, India's Asian relations have been weak.

Looking to the future, new patterns of Indian-Asian relations are coming into focus. Among those suggested by Professor Park are improved Sino-Indian ties, greater economic cooperation between Japan and India, and increased interaction between Southeast Asia and India. Clearly, India could be expected to play a greater role in Asia were it not for its domestic political economy.

The final chapter in this volume discusses some of the earlier essays and presents the views of the author, Dr. Morton I. Abramowitz. The focus is on the perceptions of the Asian actors and "how this perception might influence their interactions" and a review of the major issues relating to intra-Asian relations, issues that "will profoundly influence the peace and stability of the region." In discussing the Asian actors, Dr. Abramowitz makes a number of important points, including taking issue with Professor Barnett's stress upon the security factor as *the* concern in Chinese foreign policy and behavior. Dr. Abramowitz "would elevate domestic politics to near-paramount importance as a determinant of Chinese policy, foreign and domestic." Among the key issues that require the attention of all Asian actors are the Sino-Soviet conflict, economic relations, and internal conflict. All are serious issues in a highly volatile environment. Commenting on the Sino-Soviet conflict, Dr. Abramowitz makes an observation that might well be applied to all aspects of intra-Asian relations, namely, while there are good reasons to expect a pattern of continuity, we must not overlook the possibilities for change.

We began this review of the essays with the comment that intra-Asian relations are undergoing great changes. One is toward greater Asianization, a movement away from the politics of alliances with external sources and toward the politics of equidistance. Another theme common to the essays is the basic weaknesses of the Asian actors, politically, economically, and militarily. While new patterns of interaction are coming into focus, the future of intra-Asian relations is filled with uncertainties. There can be no question that developments in Asia are of great importance, to Asians as well as Americans. Whatever future developments may be, intra-Asian relations deserve our serious and continuous attention and study.

2. Intra-Asian Relations: An Overview

Robert A. Scalapino

In sharp contrast to the situation in Europe, interstate relations in Asia have been characterized by great volatility and an absence of any consistent pattern in recent years. The European scene may be changing. Instability in southern Europe, the uncertainties relating to American policies, and the widening divergences within East Europe could signal a troubled future. Nevertheless, the Helsinki Conference in its own fashion put an official seal upon a type of regional order that, while incomplete, partly bifurcated, and not without elements of tension, has consistently evolved in the post-1945 era. Under this order, relations between and among the states of the region have become increasingly regularized and predictable, and the threat of international conflict appears to have been reduced. In Asia, however, such developments are not a part of recent history.

Some Geopolitical Factors

Why? Geography, historical factors, political culture, and the timing of Asian development combine to give this region unique features affecting both domestic and international politics. Let us start with geography and a touch of history. In the vast area labeled "Asia" there are few well-demarcated, traditionally sanctioned ethnic-physical units. Only South

Asia as a region generally has the geographic barriers that create reasonable discrete units; here, too, significant ethnic-cultural diversity exists, cutting across modern national boundaries.

Continental Asia, now the political legacy of the great march of two empires, Russian and Chinese, is demarcated only by the vastness of its arid interior, alleviated by occasional mountain ranges, yet with few natural boundaries. If history had moved in a different direction, we would witness today a series of buffer states here, ruled by the indigenous peoples of the region—Kazakh, Uzbek, Mongol, and Tibetan. This would have made the problem of Sino-Soviet relations at once more complex and more hopeful, since buffer states between empires can serve as neutralizing zones. But this is not to be.

Similarly, the boundaries of Asia's two other major regions, Northeast and Southeast Asia, are ill-defined in geographic terms. Both are part continental, part island, and reflect a diversity of topography that has in turn affected every aspect of culture and relatively complex ethnic distribution, especially in the case of Southeast Asia. Diversity, moreover, extends within national boundaries. With Japan being a prominent exception, most such boundaries are recent and frequently the product of arbitrary political division connected with colonialism or war. Thus, the ethnic-cultural groups that coexist within current state boundaries remain largely unassimilated. Few Asian states have come close to completing what we call "the nation-building process," and the elements of alienation, separateness, and violence based upon ethnic-cultural differences bulk large in domestic politics.

The Diverse Imperial Legacies

Chinese and Indian colonialism of the pre-Western era in paradoxical fashion contributed simultaneously to a broader cultural identity and intensified divisions. The cultural reach of these two great civilizations extended further and lasted longer than their military-political controls. Almost all of Northeast Asia became a part of the Confucian world. With China as its center, this world was governed by very special concepts of interstate relations, concepts resting upon comfortable ambiguities. Suzerainty prevailed where sovereignty could not be implanted. Influence extended beyond the reach of control. Economic intercourse and social relations both served and defined political roles. The basis for political organization of a complex, extended type was laid throughout significant parts of Asia.

The Indian penetration of South and Southeast Asia took similar forms, but with different results. The social and religious impact that flowed in various waves from India was less conducive to the type of political integration related to the Confucian order. Buddhism and Hinduism, together with the Sanskrit language, created a social more than a political order, although the existence of a linkage here should not be denied. Nonetheless, the Chinese legacy, being the more secular, was also more related to those societal-wide organizational forms that serve both as prerequisites and progenitors of politicization. In some measure at least, this fitted the two empires—and their tributaries—unevenly for the political trials that lay ahead

Although no Pope existed to divide Asia, the Sino-Indian fault line ran in such a fashion as to include Annam and Tonkin in the Confucian orbit together with the whole of Northeast Asia. Laos, Cambodia, Cochin China, and the Himalayan societies, on the other hand, were more deeply influenced by the diverse traditions emanating from the Indian heartland. No simple division is possible, however, because preponderant influences shifted depending upon the era, and because some regions like Tibet long occupied an ambiguous position. Moreover, as is well known, a certain interpenetration took place between the two great civilizations, primarily in the form of the thrust of Buddhism northward.

The effect of these past empires upon the contemporary politics and international relations of Asia should not be minimized. It is to be seen not merely in terms of cultural affinities, hence communication networks, but also in the political attitudes and behavior of those elites holding power and making decisions today. Traditionalism is one of the forces that shape both the style and the substance of Chinese and Indian foreign policies at present, as well as the style and the substance of the foreign policies of neighboring states that evolved in some fashion in the shadow of these civilizations. Adjusted to modernity, such practices as the tribute system and such concepts as suzerainty live on, sometimes in contradiction to, sometimes in harmony with, Western-derived law and behavior. It is thus not surprising that in the absence of universal principles, the common institutions from whence international behavior would become regulated and routinized are lacking. And at points where traditionalism appears to recede or blend satisfactorily with the new streams, ideology threatens to take its place as a divisive force.

Meanwhile, from the seventeenth century onward, Western enclaves in Asia, harbingers of a dramatic new challenge, were superimposed on older empires. At its inception, the Western presence was not greatly different in its repercussions from the intrusion of earlier foreigners. Indeed, with respect to the masses of Asia, Western influence in the course of the next few centuries was more superficial, having only a brief period of time in which to contest deeply laid cultures. As far as the common people were concerned, the Western impact was greatest among the less cultured hill and mountain peoples, people largely bypassed in the course of earlier cultural infusions.

Among the indigenous elites, however, a very different pattern emerged. Here, over time, the Western influence was at least as great as any that had gone before it. Initially, a process of polarization ensued, with the political elite being progressively fragmented. The extremities were represented by those who wanted to struggle against everything foreign and those who were prepared to follow new paths fully. Gradually, in company with the revolutionary character of developments in the West itself, the force of new ideas gained ascendancy, threatening not merely to separate the elite from each other but also from their own society and people, hence taking from them their old identity and raison d'être.

From this impact came the process of disintegration, revolution, and attempted rebirth that has at once dominated and joined the domestic and international politics of Asia throughout the past century and more. Quite possibly, by committing itself to two disastrous wars in the first half of the twentieth century, the West ensured that the process could be all the more hastily undertaken and consummated.

In any case, in the fullness of their power, Western empires in Asia had a curious, contradictory effect. On the one hand, they bred a new "modernizing" elite over time, one proclaiming its allegiance to the broad goals of progress, nationalism, economic development, and democracy. In this, the basis for a new international order and infrastructure of communications was laid. At the same time, however, as has just been noted, "Westernism" in all its facets served to separate elites from each other and from the common man, creating in the process what has been termed "pluralist" societies, ones with growing urban-rural gaps. Its general influence was also to keep contact between one Asian society and another minimal, fostering a high degree of isolation. Put succinctly, the West gave to Asia both the tools of the future in terms of new technologies and goals, and the challenges in terms of a fragmentation and separatism that marked the domestic as well as the regional environments.

It is easy to forget, moreover, that for much of Asia, the colonial era lies in the *recent* past. Perhaps the significance of this fact is best appreciated by contrasting the timing of development of one important society, Japan, with that of most other Asian states. For reasons that are well known, Japan emerged at a very different time from its neighbors. Thus disintegration was confined largely to the decades immediately preceding the Meiji Restoration. Revolution took place in the nineteenth century, with none of the technology or ideas of the next century available. Rebirth thus followed the available models of the time, largely those of the modern oligarchic-parliamentary system—with its variants drawn from Western Europe and America.

Consequently, Japan had reached a high momentum of development by World War I. Progress, nationalism, economic growth, and democracy—all were in vogue. Japanese excess energy and power flowed into the tasks of "liberating"Asia from the twin threats of communism and Western imperialism. Total defeat once again removed Japan from active participation in the international arena after 1945 for several decades, and, of equal importance, it fixed certain new perimeters for Japanese international thought and behavior. In contrast, the developmental sequence for the rest of Asia got underway only with the events of World War II and its aftermath.

Power Relations in the Age of Decolonization

It is a distortion to label the years immediately after World War II an era of bipolarism. In fact, there was only one global power, the United States. No other nation was capable of extending its economic, political, and strategic reach throughout the world. This is not to say that Washington committed itself to all regions indiscriminately, lacking any sense of priorities. Attention from the outset was focused upon West Europe and East Asia. Nor is it to denigrate the power of the Soviet Union, a nation at once terribly wounded and in a new flush of nationalism as a result of the war. Still, these two countries were strikingly unequal in terms of power, and as American strategy could be global, that of Russia was essentially regional.

Some students have mistakenly equated this regional emphasis with defensiveness in their eagerness to establish American culpability for the Cold War. But Soviet policies of this era were defensive only in a psychological sense. The Russians did think in terms of protecting themselves from the threats—both West and East—that had repeatedly drawn them into conflict in modern times. In the mind of Stalin and many others, this required a buffer-state system in Europe and the restoration of many of the Tsarist concessions in Asia. Hence it represented an expansionist program on both sides of the Eurasian continent, with precise limits unspecified. Indeed, Marxist-Leninist rhetoric was global in its scope and possessed of a new militancy. In practical terms, however, the primary emphasis of Soviet foreign policy had to be regional, given the severe limits upon Russian strength and the clear priorities that prevailed.

Thus, Russia reached into the regions of Northeast Asia from which it had retreated nearly a half-century earlier, but it had to confine its reach largely to the continental portions. Meanwhile, the issue of an Asian continental presence was long to trouble the United States. On the one hand, the initial image of a postwar Asia held in Washington rested heavily upon a dynamic, democratic China from which much was expected. That image was also constructed out of the hope that decolonization would be both swift and peaceful, with Western-style democracies dominating South and Southeast Asia. Thus, in conceptual terms and in practical political scenarios as well, there could be no division between the Asian continent and the great island societies that existed offshore in the Western Pacific. Nevertheless, the question of the costs—and the feasibility—of a continental policy in Asia provoked American doubts at a very early point in the post-1945 era.

These doubts could only swell into strong misgivings in the years between 1945-1950. All of the initial premises held in the United States about postwar Asia proved to be in error. China slipped into deepening chaos and civil war, and toward communism. Decolonization proved to be more complex and costly to all parties in some regions than had been envisaged, and the results were often disappointing from the perspective of Washington. The factors shifting the political balance within Asia, moreover, seemed uniquely unsusceptible to U.S. power in its conventional forms.

Nevertheless, when the first great postwar upheaval had ended, Asia fell largely into three parts: the communist states, deeply under Soviet influence in domestic and foreign policies alike; the U.S. bloc, where the American imprimatur was strongly felt; and the "nonaligned" states, self-consciously defining their position as outside either the Soviet or American orbits.

These aspects of this first era after the war stand out. First, alliances tended to be exclusive, all-encompassing, and permitting limited flexibility. There were, to be sure, men like Syngman Rhee who proved unruly, and the American style of politics permitted far more of this than the Soviet system. In any case, however, communications across alliances within Asia were exceedingly limited.

Second, this was a highly ideological, hence moralistic period on all sides. The United States, shocked by developments in East Europe and, later, by events in China and Korea, managed to keep a consensus regarding foreign policy rare in peacetime by defining the struggle as one for human and national freedom. The communists turned their full ire against "imperialism," racism, and "capitalist exploitation." The nonaligned leaders issued statements surfeited with self-righteousness, statements that seemed hypocritical or romantic to both of the camps to which they were directed. From this moralism, consensus was built or maintained on all sides, but by the same token, the processes of dialogue and compromise, while never wholly absent, were stunted and fragile. In these terms, the Cold War has merit as a term, although like most catchphrases, it fails to capture the underlying complexity of the era.

Finally, Asian interstate relations were almost nonexistent, particularly in the early post-1945 period. The international politics of the period was dominated by the United States and the USSR. Japan, once close to hegemony over East Asia and a profoundly revolutionary force upon Asia both in victory and in defeat, was now strictly isolated from others. China, first in civil war, then in the throes of a communist-directed revolution, restricted its contacts largely to the Soviet Union and other European communist states until the end of the Stalin era, its intervention in Korea being the sole major exception. Southern Asia was almost totally preoccupied with the issues of independence. Only India sought in some measure to act as the spokesman for the "emerging world," parlaying the moral-political authority of Indian leadership into areas where Indian military-economic power could not reach. Before China, it should always be remembered, there was India.

Thus, to the extent that a political-military equilibrium was fashioned in Asia, it was still essentially the product of external forces, with Asian societies, new and old, playing a quite minimal role. The United States, drawing from its massive largess, was the major actor, providing for much of East Asia a Pax Americana and influencing domestic institutions as well as foreign policies.

Bandung, it might be argued, was a turning point, a signal that an Asian international order cutting across ideological lines and only minimally dependent upon Western power involvement was conceivable. But in another sense, Bandung was possible only because of the embryonic character of Asian development. Its high level of generality betokened the largely unfocused sense of national interest still marking the emerging states of this area, their general military weakness, and the absence of any established patterns of behavior in an international environment in which deep divisions were accompanied by that extensive isolation that grew out of the recent past.

As these conditions changed within Asia, the significance of Bandung diminished, with a quality of unreality surrounding its afterglow. Bandung increasingly appeared as a form of pageantry without substance, a final act of childhood innocence. Peaceful coexistence, the most promising concept to emerge from the conference, was not to be realized through speeches or pledges but only potentially through a multiple, complex process of evolution that extended into the uncertain future.

Stability and Change in the Balance-of-Power Era

On either side of Bandung in time, two events provided the basis for the transitional era of the 1960s, namely, the Korean

War and the Sino-Soviet cleavage. The Korean War, essentially a product of communist miscalculation of American
intentions, signaled the potential weaknesses in America's
Asian policies—above all, the impossibility of an open,
democratic society fighting a protracted, limited war anywhere without risking deep and irreconcilable fissures at
home; the risks also of a forward continental policy raising
profound anxieties on the part of massive, neighboring
nations; and the challenges implicit in working intimately
with a non-Western, emerging society and seeking to redirect
its political culture in profoundly revolutionary ways.

All of these issues were to be raised in an even more acute
form at a later point in Vietnam. In both instances, the
evidence permits no doubt that the communists took the
initiative in seeking to resolve the complex issue of a divided
state by resort to force and that the United States, in company
with indigenous noncommunists, sought to contain the
communist drive, proclaiming the issue to be whether this
form of aggression would be allowed to succeed (the patterns
of the 1930s were clearly in mind). None of these facts
obviated the difficulties noted above, however, and from
these difficulties were ultimately to come the frustrations
and defeat of such significance to a later period.

Within a few years after the inconclusive end of the Korean
War, it was the turn of the Soviet Union to face its most
profound postwar trauma. The widening breach between
Russia and China, the product of many factors, was at root a
conflict between two intensely nationalistic, strongly committed, highly authoritarian elites, who might share a
common ideology but who had different cultural roots,
timings of development, degrees of power, and hence substantially different senses of national interest.

Whatever the future may hold, the Sino-Soviet split has
fundamentally changed the nature of Asian intrastate relations, noncommunist as well as communist. One cannot
view this event in isolation, to be sure. The wider impact of
the Sino-Soviet cleavage unfolded slowly and in a context
where events of near-equal significance were transpiring. As

we have noted, the United States had committed its prestige in Indochina, and the issue of American credibility was to loom ever larger, first with allies, later with the "neutrals," and finally, with the major communist powers.

Finally, the transitional fifteen years after 1960 have witnessed the emergence of all remaining parts of Southern Asia as either politically independent entities or as territories incorporated into some Asian state—with only the most minor exceptions. This has clearly meant no absence of continuing problems, as was signaled at the outset of this essay. Whether each of these states deserves to be considered a nation remains debatable. The role of external Western powers, nonetheless, has receded everywhere, albeit not uniformly.

What has been the impact of these events in the broadest terms? The first and clearest result has been a trend toward Asianization, a movement toward the more intricate and intensive involvement of the Asian states with each other—in harmony or in conflict. In this process, the role of the Soviet Union in particular is rendered more complex, since the USSR is both an external and an internal force insofar as Asia is concerned. Nor can one be certain yet of the point at which American commitments will stabilize, given the extensive nature of American interests in the contemporary Asian scene and given its territorial possessions in the Western Pacific. Taking a different perspective, Japan, indisputably an Asian society, is also one of the world's two global economic powers, and hence it has concerns—and policies—that extend far beyond Asia. It can thus allow its immediate environment to shape only a portion of its policies. These caveats having been set forth, however, the fact remains that Asianization has progressed at an accelerating pace, adding many new complications to the interstate relations of the area.

Second, there has been an unmistakable trend away from exclusive alliances and toward the politics of equidistance. Let the word *toward* be emphasized because the mechanical application of equidistance is not possible, even if it were thought desirable. Nevertheless, wherever one looks in Asia today, the old exclusive, all-encompassing alliances are giving way to new arrangements. Even where "special ties" continue to have their greatest validity—as in the case of U.S.-Japanese relations—new elements of flexibility and separateness have made their presence felt.

Most of the small nations of Asia have been strongly affected by the new order. Their search has been for a position that affords contact with all parties of significance, yet with some economic, political, or military relations tailored specifically to their particular position. In this fashion, the channels of communication have been broadened; at the same time, an effort has been made to retain or establish those special ties that seem either essential or beneficial.

Inevitably, such policies have introduced a strong element of pragmatism into policies that once seemed governed heavily by ideological constraints. Who would have predicted a decade ago that South Korea would be ardently soliciting contact with both the USSR and the PRC while the North Koreans sought to obtain recognition from Japan and the United States? Who would have foreseen that the Chinese would ultimately exhort the United States to regain its consensus and retain its military strength so as to meet the Soviet global challenge?

In sum, with the progressive breakdown of the early postwar alliance system, each Asian nation—large and small—has had to reposition itself in the light of the new fluid and complex patterns of power. Thus, for Japan, the simplicities of total dependence upon the United States have given way to "special ties" coupled with a growing independence, and an effort to "normalize" and expand relations with both the PRC and the USSR. Ideally, as the Japanese are well aware, the relations with the two major communist states should be in some degree of equilibrium. Any pronounced, uniform tilt would deeply antagonize the neglected party and also limit Japanese flexibility. Yet experience has shown Japan how very difficult it is to effectuate the politics of equidistance, and up to now, the Japanese have found themselves increasingly squeezed between conflicting pressures in a most uncomfortable fashion.

In Southeast Asia also, with some exceptions, the trend has been toward equidistance. In the aftermath of American defeat, such former allies as Thailand and the Philippines, together with Malaysia, moved to adjust their relations with the PRC, having earlier established ties with the USSR (except in the case of the Philippines). Once again, however, an optimal position has proven difficult to achieve. Despite surface indications of forgiveness and cordiality toward these wayward nations, China continues to ride two horses. Although state-to-state relations improve, comrade-to-comrade relations are not abandoned. Thus, ties with the underground guerrilla communist movements of Southeast Asia clearly continue, as do certain types of assistance. Long ago, Burma—a state that has cultivated neutralism to the point of near-total isolation—discovered similar facts to its bewilderment and sorrow. As one result, the newcomers to equidistance are restrained from severing old security ties completely, even though the validity of these ties has been brought into increasing doubt. Economic pulls can promote a degree of alignment too.

For the Asian communist states as well, equidistance is at once an attractive concept and one difficult to realize. Vietnam presumably has no desire to run the risks of confrontation with its massive Chinese neighbor, but it nevertheless faces a growing set of issues that could lead to that end, from jurisdictional problems relating to the South China Sea islands to the broader question of who shall exert primary influence within continental Southeast Asia. Peking has openly challenged Hanoi with respect to the islands, refrained from giving economic support to a needy and requesting client, and shown every sign of putting the Vietnamese government into a category close to that of the Indians, privately, if not publicly. At this point, in reaction, Hanoi leans sharply toward the Soviet bloc and carries Laos in this direction as well.

North Korea, on the other hand, having had indifferent-to-poor relations with the Soviet Union for nearly two decades, tilts in the opposite direction despite its continued dependence upon Russian military and industrial goods, a dependence it is now seeking to lessen. The same is true of Cambodia. The Khmers' fear of Vietnamese power, moreover, can be found also in Thailand, amid uncertainties as to whether China is prepared or willing to offset any Vietnamese thrust. For Singapore and Indonesia, on the other hand, it is the specter of a rising PRC influence throughout the region that has given pause and, indeed, this thought is not far from the minds of all Southeast Asian leaders, at least as a middle-range prospect.

The thrust toward equidistance, therefore, has been accompanied by various doubts and setbacks, promoting either the maintenance of, or the reversion to, some degree of alignment. This alignment, however, is not alliance. Rather, its essence is captured in the less exclusive concept of a tilt—a concept suggesting a capacity for relatively rapid change, a new element of flexibility, and a growing complexity befitting a very uncertain, transitional period.

Toward a Balance of Weakness?

In the broadest sense, however, a new reliance seems to be gaining ground, namely, a reliance upon a balance of weakness. First, let us pay homage to select strengths, especially among the large states. Two of the three major powers of the Pacific-Asian region, Russia and China, certainly have as one goal a greater strategic-political role in Asia, and both are currently making an effort to expand their military reach as well as to increase their productive capacities.

Meanwhile, the United States remains the strongest nation in the world in material terms, and one whose economic and political interests in Asia are growing in many respects rather than declining. Moreover, a substantial number of Asian states, as has been noted, are urging a reconstitution of the American will so that the U.S. presence and power will not precipitously disappear from Asia.

Nor can one ignore the unique role of Japan, a nation still grappling with recession but one whose economic power shapes the course of many societies around it.

Having made these points and conceding others of a similar nature, however, let us analyze the elements of weakness, commencing with the USSR. Above all, Russia remains a very foreign force in Asia, its physical presence in the very center of that continent notwithstanding. Russian culture is largely unsuited to assimilation, and its developmental program is a dubious model for most Asian societies. Moreover, it has a very mixed record of diplomatic performance, one not noted for flexibility, subtlety, or finesse.

The Soviet Union, moreover, while possessing some important negotiatory instruments in the form of unexploited resources, especially in the Asian portions of the USSR, and a formidable military capability, also faces the likelihood of rising pressures from within its own society for a larger share of the material goods produced. Consumer demand within this nation has only begun to manifest itself, but it will certainly grow, a product of elitist as well as mass desires.

In broader political-cultural terms as well, can changes not be expected? Essentially, the Soviet Union is a porous society today, increasingly susceptible to the influence of West and East Europe with the isolation of centuries giving way at a progressive rate to interactions that over time even a highly authoritarian government may be less and less able to control. This is not to advance a concept of convergence, an oversimplified notion, but it is to suggest the inevitability of new currents entering into Russia in a steady stream, mixing with those changes concomitant with Soviet internal development to make this a more differentiated society.

The combination of these factors may be offset by the steady growth of the Soviet Union's military power. In all probability the USSR will be much stronger militarily in Asia a decade hence than it is today, in conventional as much as in nuclear weapons. Thus, it will be in a position to defend its positions and, quite possibly, to expand its influence. But even if this is the case, will it be possible to utilize this military power to alter or control the politics of Asia, and over what perimeters, and at what cost? Put differently, can the Soviet Union acquire the mix of political, economic, and military capability that will render the risks and costs of power extension acceptable in the middle and long run?

Whatever may be the case a decade hence, it is not clear that the Soviet Union feels that it can now induce changes in the Asian scene that would be to its advantage. Naturally, leadership changes in both China and North Korea are strongly desired, but the Russian capacity to influence such changes in any favorable manner is questionable. Other changes, for example, the unification of Korea, the annexation of Taiwan by the PRC, or even major changes in Southeast Asia—with the possible exception of a growing Vietnamese empire—would not be of current advantage to the USSR. In certain respects, therefore, Moscow has good reason to support the status quo, and the Asian collective security concept, strongly advanced by Russia, being a counterpart to its European model, betokens that fact. It is an essentially negative objective—the containment of China—toward which Soviet energies are currently directed in Asia, and that could well continue to be the primary Soviet preoccupation for the foreseeable future.

The weaknesses of China are of a different order. In the first place, they stem from the prodigious challenges of "modernizing" the most populous, and one of the most backward, nations in the world. Even if recent growth rates can be maintained, the task of raising the Chinese people well above marginal survival levels is a task of decades.

Meanwhile, as recent events have so dramatically indicated, political instability remains a strong probability. The end of the Mao-Chou era leaves weak institutions and strong personalities—a dangerous combination. No one can predict whether Chinese political instability can be confined to elitist circles, leaving productivity and the basic political order unaffected, as has been the case recently, or whether it will lap over into the mass arena, as during the Cultural Revolution. But few would assert that we have seen the last political upheaval within China's ruling circles.

Behind these upheavals, of course, lies something more than mere struggles for power or personality clashes. This is a society rife with a series of complex issues centering upon the problem of combining revolution and development. China's rhetoric is Marxist-Leninist-Maoist, but its goals are those of the Meiji Restoration—to be a rich and powerful nation by the end of the twentieth century. To the extent that revolution and development go together, the fundamental issue does not emerge, but to the extent that they diverge, the issue is joined, especially in this era when a first- and second-generation revolutionary elite still cling tenaciously to the top rungs of power.

There can be little doubt, therefore, that despite China's ambitions to recreate for itself the role of the Central Kingdom and, in its special way, to develop both a sphere of influence and a client or buffer-state system, the resolution of China's developmental problems may in some measure restrict or inhibit a forward foreign policy.

Nor can one overlook the fact that where the People's Republic of China is a near presence and where the overseas Chinese community is a formidable element of power, anti-Chinese sentiment lies always close to the political surface, cultural proximities notwithstanding. Fear can bring acquiescence or accommodation, but resentment also evokes resistance, sometimes in subtle ways. This the Chinese face in various parts of Asia, with ideological lines being of limited meaning when ethnic-cultural or nationalist sentiments are exploited.

There remains, moreover, a deep schizophrenia in China's Asian policies, as noted earlier, with state-to-state, people-to-people, and comrade-to-comrade relations operating simultaneously, providing both positive and negative elements for the Chinese image.

The weaknesses of the United States, since they are the

most publicized, are the most apparent. On the one hand, the direct commitment of American military power, at least in a protracted, limited war, has been proven to exact a prohibitively high political price, given the nature of American society. But since many aspects of American culture are at least as foreign to much of Asia as those of the Soviet Union, it is by no means clear that other forms of influence can be successful. What can be applied from the American model at this juncture? In political-ideological terms, the movement is away from the liberal, politically open society throughout the world, with Asia a part of the vanguard. This raises the question of whether the broadest economic and political trends will make possible the type of base from which meaningful political alliances or mutually benefical economic relationships can ensue.

The negative impact of these problems, moreover, can be quite as great upon the American people as upon others, and unlike the people of the USSR or China, they can make their opposition or reservations emphatically clear to those in charge of making and executing policies. The absence of a consensus supporting American foreign policy is not new. Indeed, it was a pronounced characteristic of the troubled interwar period from 1919 to 1941. In that era, however, the United States did not cast the shadow over world events that it has since 1945. The apprehensions that have swept over the globe recently concerning American instability and division have been particularly manifest in Asia, and they have come from such diverse sources as the People's Republic of China and the Republic of Korea—to pick merely two examples from the political spectrum.

Finally, we may look at Japan. The recent energy crisis coupled with the global recession revealed the other side of the Japanese miracle, namely, an economy uniquely affected by international events and, hence, uniquely dependent upon the broadest possible access to markets and upon global conditions of peace. These facts reinforce Japan's efforts to separate economics and politics in its foreign policies. Such efforts in turn, when united with the new political culture of the past thirty years, provide major obstacles to any restoration of a high-posture, power-oriented diplomacy.

One certainly cannot rule out a reversion. Should some combination of perceived threat and the full loss of American credibility develop, the nationalist proclivities of the Japanese, now reemerging, might assert themselves in new directions. In a very broad sense, however, the Japanese cycle of development has given militancy not merely an aura of defeat but one of being passé. This appears to be the age of the continental mass society; the era when small nations possessed of great overseas empires could govern the destinies of vast numbers of people is now merely a part of history. Nor does the growing political instability of Japan suggest a strong capacity for Asian leadership.

When these weaknesses of the major Pacific-Asian societies have been surveyed, what conclusions is one entitled to draw? Perhaps two lines can be set forth, each with opposite implications. The "optimistic" scenario would be as follows. Large-scale conflict between the major societies is less probable for two reasons: the costs of such conflict in a nuclear age and the impossibility of "victory" because of the complexities of the current international situation as well as the internal weaknesses of each society (which a general war could only extenuate). In recent times, it should be noted, only the United States could truly afford to win a general war, and American capacities to cope with victory in the future are clearly limited.

The unlikelihood of a general war does not carry to the local or regional levels, it is admitted. Intrastate and interstate conflict of a localized nature can be granted as a future probability, even inevitability. Yet while these conflicts will cause intense local suffering in certain instances and will involve some degree of external involvement, a "natural threshold" of containment will emerge, capable of preventing any progression toward large-scale conflict even of a regional character. This will be true again because each actor will perceive the costs involved and because of the sheer

complexity of relations beyond the internal or bilateral
levels. Asianization has had this result among others. Thus,
a new type of limited war will fix the outer perimeters of
politics when there has been an escalation to the level of
force.

Under these conditions, some degree of equidistance will
be possible for both major and minor powers, and no single
state will exercise hegemony over any appreciable region
beyond its own borders. Gradually, moreover, under these
conditions, regionalism will take more coherent forms, with
certain suprastate institutions being established and
strengthened. Regionalism, indeed, will become the central
gravitational pull in the international politics of the late
twentieth century. This will bring a certain benefit to China
as far as Asia is concerned, but full hegemony will be denied
Peking because of the existence of other important Asian
powers and the extraordinary complexity of the Asian scene.

In sum, out of the pervasiveness of weakness and the
growth of complexity in the global political milieu will
ensue a set of restraints playing a role that substitutes in
some degree for the role played by an earlier balance of power
in containing (not eliminating) violence and restricting
influence to more localized and regional levels. Subtly, the
shift is now taking place from the psychological play of
positive (power) to negative (cost) forces as key factors in
restraint. This in turn will gradually lead to new institutions
of a suprastate type and, at the same time, induce support for
some experiments cutting across regional lines.

There is another scenario, much less promising from an
American perspective, that could be advanced. Weaknesses
are no more susceptible to a stable international equilibrium than strengths. Under present circumstances, moreover, they operate generally to the disadvantage of a society
such as the United States. At the heart of the American
problem is the increasing difficulty that a politically open
society, however powerful, faces in developing the consensus
necessary to carry out protracted, incremental policies
successfully—whether they involve negotiations or conflict.

Hence, the world order that was based upon American capacity and commitment to a very significant degree is now moving into history.

No new order, however, will emerge quickly or easily to take its place, and the transitional period is rife with dangers. This does not necessarily mean the advent of nuclear war, but the capacity to use military threats effectively is shifting to states and movements with highly structured, authoritarian infrastructures. It is quite probable that for the period directly ahead some combination of violence and the threat of violence will dominate the international politics of the Asian region; a combination of cooperation and accommodation is unlikely.

Regionalism will thus not be very effective except as it is enforced by a superior power, especially given the absence of common values and institutions. Interstate relations in Asia will continue to be characterized by irregularity, a lack of international safeguards, and a minimum of common purpose. Peaceful coexistence will remain rhetoric, with reality resting upon the frequent, if not constant, interference of one state in the internal affairs of another. This interference will take many forms—from sustained efforts to influence leadership and policies, and arms transfers on a large scale, to various forms of activities in alliance with indigenous antistate forces.

Under these conditions, miscalculations or involvement in "civil" conflicts could bring about a major-power confrontation despite the risks and costs. This would probably not take the form of a declared war; it would sooner be an escalation of violence that directly involved two or more states. Even within a strictly regional context, moreover, such issues as resource control, boundaries, and similar problems might evoke direct major-power participation in an Asian conflict.

It is possible that the future in fact holds some combination of these two "pure" alternatives, or that there will be a tendency for a degree of oscillation between them. Whatever the outcome, however, it is the paradox of weakness in the midst of unprecedented productivity and military power that casts its shadow over the future of Asian international relations today. This, together with the type of international complexity that makes each additional commitment geometric in its costs, may provide growing restraints in the coming era.

This is in no sense to relegate power, including military power, to a position of insignificance. It is rather to suggest that the elements of weakness—in their own unequal and changing forms—will increasingly vie with those of strength in shaping national behavior and hence interstate relations in a period when the latter are insufficient to underwrite a stable international order.

3. China and the Balance of Power in Asia

A. Doak Barnett

Since the late 1960s, the far-reaching changes that have taken place in China's foreign policies and international relationships, paralleling important changes in the policies and positions of the other major powers in East Asia, have profoundly altered the basic pattern of international relations in the region. The development of a bitter military confrontation between China and the Soviet Union and the intense competition between these two powers throughout East Asia (and worldwide), the limited détente between Peking and Washington, and full normalization of Sino-Japanese relations rapidly and dramatically altered the basic configuration of big-power relations in the region between 1968 and 1972. During this same period, the United States' disengagement from the Indochinese states and its moves to reduce its military presence elsewhere in Asia, the Soviet Union's efforts to step up its diplomatic, economic, and naval activities in the region, and Japan's steady expansion of its economic influence also had far-reaching effects. The result has been the emergence of a new kind of four-power

This essay appeared as "Peking and the Asian Power Balance," in *Problems of Communism* 15, no. 4 (July-August 1976):36-48.

pattern of relationships among the major powers, to which all the smaller nations in the region have been compelled to adjust in varying ways and degrees.

Although, as indicated, changes in the policies of all four major powers have helped to create this new situation, it is clear that shifts in Peking's foreign policy strategy have been fundamental in transforming the nature of the international balance in the region. Many of these shifts have appeared to involve dramatic reversals of past policies, and the seeming suddenness of some of them has startled world opinion. Inevitably, they have posed a variety of questions about the basic motivations and objectives underlying Peking's foreign policies.

When and why did China's leaders decide to adopt what seemed to be a radically new overall foreign policy strategy? Are Peking's new policies likely to continue unchanged into the indefinite future, or are further major changes possible or likely? What variables are likely to work for continuity, or for change, in Chinese policies in the period immediately ahead? What can one deduce from Peking's recent policy shifts about fundamental Chinese priorities and goals in dealing with the outside world?

The Military-Security Factor

It is obvious to any student of Peking's foreign policies that there is no single key to an understanding of what the Chinese communists' basic approach to foreign affairs is. China's policies, like those of other nations, are shaped by a multiplicity of attitudes, forces, and factors. Ideological beliefs clearly have a significant influence on the Chinese leaders' world views and strategic prescriptions, expecially regarding long-term goals. So, too, do historically rooted cultural attitudes and the intense nationalist feelings that have moved all modern Chinese leaders. Many of Peking's policies can best be understood as quite pragmatic, *ad hoc* attempts to pursue very limited and immediate national interests and to enhance in a very general way China's international influence. Some Chinese policies represent deliberate initiatives taken by Peking's leaders. Many, however, are essentially reactive; Chinese leaders, like leaders elsewhere, spend much of their time and energy determining how to respond to actions taken by others—that is, deciding how to cope with external pressures and forces impinging on them from the changing international environment. Domestic politics and debates determine many foreign policy decisions in China, as elsewhere. So, too, do economic imperatives and the changing views within the Chinese leadership on how best to achieve their development goals.

Analysis of the Chinese communists' approach to international affairs must take full account of the multiplicity of such factors that influence particular policies; when realities are complex, there is no virtue in ignoring the complexities. However, it is also important to try to understand what Chinese priorities are, to assess what weight Peking gives to different concerns and objectives (especially when various goals appear to be in conflict), and to try to judge what factors have been the primary determinants of the major shifts that have periodically taken place in Peking's overall foreign policy strategy.

The central thesis of this brief essay is that, although ideology clearly influences Chinese communist leaders' perceptions of the world, and of how to deal with it, in important ways, and although many economic and other interests shape particular Chinese policies, the primary factors determining Peking's most important decisions on overall foreign policy strategy are related above all to their military-security concerns, viewed in a broad geopolitical context. The major shifts in China's overall foreign policy can best be understood, therefore, in terms of changes in the Peking leaders' perception of external threats and in their strategic decisions on how best to cope with such threats.[1]

In the late 1960s, for example, the crucial factor influencing Chinese policy was the deterioration of Sino-Soviet relations to the point of possible military conflict, a development that lead Peking's leaders to conclude—apparently during 1968-1969—that the Russians now posed a greater and more immediate danger to China's security than the Americans did. The Chinese leaders' opening to the United States and their normalization of relations with Japan, as well as important adjustments they made in policies toward both Northeast and Southeast Asia, followed logically from that conclusion.

More than is generally recognized, moreover, military-security factors were the critical ones at key stages in the development of the Sino-Soviet conflict from the late 1950s on. Much of the writing on the Sino-Soviet conflict, especially in the 1960s, focused on the ideological differences between Peking and Moscow. There is no doubt that ideological—as well as cultural, economic, and many other—factors must be taken fully into account in any comprehensive analysis of how the Sino-Soviet dispute evolved over the years. On balance, however, the evidence we now have suggests that the most important Sino-Soviet differences were precipitated by conflicts over military-security issues.

In my view, there were three crucial turning points in the Sino-Soviet conflict, each of which qualitatively changed relationships between the two countries. The first was during 1957-1959. These years witnessed a divergence of broad Soviet and Chinese strategies toward the United States. Moscow moved toward a coexistence policy (or what would now be called détente) vis-á-vis Washington, and Peking feared that this would seriously compromise important Chinese national interests—in the Taiwan area and elsewhere—which the Chinese leaders at that time believed to require a confrontation policy toward the United States. The crisis resulting from Peking's bombardment of the Chinese Nationalist–held island of Quemoy in 1958 made clear to the Chinese communists the limits of the assistance the Russians were prepared to give them under the Sino-Soviet alliance; it also heightened Soviet anxieties that the Chinese could involve the USSR in military conflicts that Moscow wished to stay out of. In this same period, disputes over naval issues further highlighted Sino-Soviet differences on basic military-security questions. Finally, in 1959, soon after the disagreements over the offshore island crisis and naval issues, Moscow ended its aid to China's nuclear weapons development program—clearly a major blow to Peking. The net effect of these developments was to convince Chinese leaders that the Sino-Soviet alliance was of limited utility to them (and to create doubts about the alliance in Moscow as well).[2] (Peking's 1960 ideological offensive against Moscow, it should be noted, followed rather preceded these developments.)

The second major turning point was in 1962-1963. Again, basic differences focused on nuclear issues. When the Russians moved toward agreement with the Americans on a limited nuclear test-ban treaty, the Chinese requested Moscow not to go through with it.[3] The Russians, however, chose to do so anyway, and the Chinese regarded this as an act of Soviet-American collusion aimed primarily at them. From Peking's perspective, the signing of the agreement was probably a "point of no return" symbolizing the end, for all practical purposes, of the Sino-Soviet pact as an operative military alliance. (Again, Peking's intensification of ideological debate with Moscow followed rather than preceded a major falling-out on concrete policy issues. In 1963-1964, the Chinese brought many previous policy disagreements touching upon concrete national interests into the open.)

The third major turning point converted the long-developing rift between Peking and Moscow from a political conflict into a military confrontation. From the Chinese perspective, the combination of the Soviet military buildup around China from 1965 on, Moscow's intervention in Czechoslovakia in 1968, and the Sino-Soviet border clashes in 1969 raised the possibility that Moscow might be considering a military attack on China.[4] Moreover, Peking's leaders probably felt that even if Moscow was not planning to attack, it was nevertheless pursuing a hostile policy of military-backed pressure on China (similar, in Chinese eyes, to American policy during the Dulles era). Their conclusion, clearly, was that China's priority immediate foreign policy objective should be to do everything possible to deter any Soviet attack and to try to build new counterweights to check the growth of Soviet influence—first of all in East Asia, but worldwide as well. The decisions to open relations with the United States (which was seen as a nation whose power had peaked and begun to wane[5]) and to normalize relations with Japan (which was seen as a prime target of Soviet efforts to encircle China in both a political and a broad strategic sense[6]) were accompanied by significant shifts in Chinese policy toward both Northeast Asia and Southeast Asia.

Peking's primary immediate preoccupation in both of these areas now was competition with Moscow for influence, rather than competition with Washington. The Chinese position regarding Japanese-American security ties changed fundamentally; instead of denouncing the US-Japan security treaty, the Chinese now endorsed it.[7] With respect to Korea, Peking, in order to outdo Moscow, increased its political support of Pyongyang against Seoul and Washington, although it apparently continued at the same time to exercise a restraining hand on Kim Il Sung to discourage him from military adventurism.[8] In Southeast Asia, Chinese fear of increased Soviet influence (and, to a lesser extent, of increased North Vietnamese influence as well)—especially in the Indochina area—led Peking to do all it could to outbid the Russians in a struggle for influence, but its efforts have had only mixed results. During 1975, although Cambodia adopted a definitely pro-Peking stance, new strains developed in relations between Peking and Hanoi (which tilted slightly toward Moscow), and Laos tried to balance its relations with both the major communist powers and Vietnam.[9] Elsewhere, in noncommunist Southeast Asia, China deemphasized (without abandoning) the revolutionary component in its policies, instead stressing normalized state-to-state relations with Malaysia, the Philippines, and Thailand.[10] Beyond establishing diplomatic ties, it also made clear that under existing circumstances—i.e., the potential threat that it now sees the Soviet Union as posing in the area—it tacitly approves of continuing security relationships between noncommunist Southeast Asian nations and the United States.[11] Now, Peking repeatedly warns that one should not, while expelling a wolf from the front door, let a tiger in the back door.

The New Strategic World View

In light of these and other changes in Chinese policies, as well as in broad international alignments affecting the region, it is not suprising that Peking has been impelled to redefine publicly its overall strategic world view and to try to explain its new policies, and justify them, to skeptics in China. The most dramatic official statement of that strategic world view was contained in Teng Hsiao-p'ing's 1974 UN speech, which analyzed global affairs in terms of three worlds.[12] Teng identified the two superpowers as the First World, the other industrialized nations as the Second World, and the developing nations in Asia, Africa, and Latin America as the Third World. The most important struggle in the world, he asserted, is that between the Third World and the First, with support for the Third World to be expected from the Second on some issues. Teng also proclaimed what had been implicit in Peking's policy for some time—namely, that in the Chinese view the socialist camp no longer exists and China now belongs to the Third World.

This new schema (which in some respects is the logical culmination of long-developing trends in Chinese policy that had led to a steadily increasing identification with the developing nations on China's part) reveals important aspects of Peking's current approach to what it calls a world of "turbulence and unrest." It is also, however, quite misleading in many respects. Despite their current stress on the political importance of the Third World, Chinese leaders are still concerned, above all, with potential threats to their security and with the need to create effective counterweights to such threats. As they now view their security problems in a broad geopolitical context, their perceptions of the current distribution of military-relevant power appear to be very similar in some respects to the views articulated by Richard

Nixon and Henry Kissinger in 1971-1972—namely that there
are really five major power centers that can play key roles in
the current balance in the world: the Soviet Union, the
United States, Western Europe, China, and Japan. To judge
by Peking's actual foreign policy behavior, as well as by
many Chinese leaders' statements (especially private statements), the central task of all the latter four, as Peking sees it,
is—or should be—to check the spread of Soviet influence.
The Chinese leaders' actions, in short, suggest that they
recognize that, in relation to immediate security problems,
the industrial nations are far more important than the
developing nations. Moreover, Peking does not, in reality,
treat the two superpowers as a unit but instead distinguishes
fairly clearly between them, arguing that the contradictions
between the two are "irreconcilable" and explicitly or tacitly
supporting U.S. positions in most conflict situations where
American and Soviet interests clash.

In sum, Peking now appears to base its policies on two
different conceptualizations: on one hand, its publicly articulated three-world schema, in which both superpowers are
labeled adversaries; and, on the other, its unstated view of
five major power centers, in which the United States is
regarded as a limited "ally" against the Soviet Union.
Although overlapping to some extent, these two world views
are very different in their implications and involve inevitable
"contradictions." Both are important, since each reveals the
basis for certain aspects of Chinese policy. But the unstated
view is by far the more important of the two, at least for the
immediate future, because it is more directly relevant to
Peking's pressing concerns about China's security problems
and to current Maoist thinking on the best way to cope with
these problems.

In many respects, a careful examination of what Peking
actually does is more helpful to an understanding of its basic
strategic approach to China's security problems than an
exegesis of its public programmatic statements. Nevertheless, there are several official statements, some published in
China and some not, that are extremely revealing with

regard to the strategic premises and assumptions underlying the current approach of Chinese leaders to their priority foreign policy problems. Here it will suffice to cite only two: Mao's 1940 directive "On Policy," which was republished—with commentary emphasizing its contemporary relevance—in 1971 (after Kissinger's visit to China and before Nixon had come to Peking);[13] and a classified document entitled "Outline of Education on Situation for Companies," which was issued by a Yunnan People's Liberation Army Political Department in April 1973 for use in indoctrinating PLA men (a copy of this document was obtained by the Chinese Nationalists and published in 1974).[14]

"On Policy" is a very revealing exposition of Mao's basic strategic approach to the problem of coping with the main threat facing China and the Communist Party at any particular time. This approach, which crystallized during the war against Japan, embodies a distinctive balance-of-power strategy based on united front concepts. The Chinese Communist Party, Mao said in "On Policy," must follow a "revolutionary dual policy." It must draw distinctions between various sorts of enemies (identifying the main one at any time) and also between different sorts of "allies." "We build our policy on these distinctions," he declared. It is essential, he emphasized, to maintain "independence and initiative"; nevertheless, "our basic line is to use all possible foreign help, subject to the principle of independent prosecution of the war and reliance on our own efforts." However, in building a united front, the party should pursue a policy that is "neither all alliance, but [which] combines alliance and struggle," it should be a policy of "uniting with [potential allies], in so far as they are still in favor of resisting" the main enemy and "isolating them, in so far as they are determined to oppose" us. "Our tactics," he stressed, "are guided by . . . the . . . principle: to make use of contradictions, win over the many, oppose the few, and crush our enemies one by one."

The 1971 commentary, written at the time of the republication of "On Policy," was designed to use the concepts elaborated in that document to explain and justify China's current moves in the direction of an opening toward the United States, and it made explicit certain basic points that had been implicit but not directly stated in the original. "Chairman Mao," said the commentary, "most clearly distinguished between the primary enemy and the secondary and between the temporary allies and the indirect allies." His "tactical principles" involved "a dialectical unity of firm principles and great flexibility" and explicated "the art of waging all kinds of struggles in a flexible way" so as to "isolate the primary enemy." The commentary also stressed that "the dual policy of alliance and struggle is built on the dual character of all allies in the united front."

The secret Yunnan document issued in 1973 analyzed China's strategic problems in even more explicit terms, applying the kind of Maoist concepts outlined in "On Policy" to the concrete situation of the 1970s. "The two archenemies facing us are U.S. imperialism and Soviet revisionism," it said.

> We are to fight for the overthrow of these two enemies. This has already been written into the new party constitution. Nevertheless, are we to fight these two enemies simultaneously, using the same might? No. Are we to ally ourselves with one against the other? Definitely not. We act in light of changes in situations, tipping the scale diversely at different times. But where is our main point of attack, and how are we to exploit their contradictions? This involves a high level of tactics.

It is then stated, bluntly, that today "Soviet revisionism is our country's most threatening enemy," which "has been trying to control us and subvert us and destroy us"; moreover, it added "in terms of geographical positions, Soviet revisionism abuts on China. From this point of view, its threat to our country is much greater than that of the United States and much more direct." Comparing the United States and the Soviet Union, it said:

the present situation is: US imperialism's counterrevolutionary global strategy has met with repeated setbacks; its aggressive power has been weakened; and hence, it has had to make some retraction and adjustment of its strategy. Soviet revisionism, on the other hand, is stretching its arms in all directions and is expanding desperately. It is more crazy, adventurist and deceptive. That is why Soviet revisionism has become our country's most dangerous and most important enemy.

The document denounced "some comrades" who "slander and vilify us, saying that our talks with the United States meant a 'collusion between China and the United States,' an 'alliance with the United States against the Soviet Union,' etc." Such people have a "low ability to make distinctions"; in reality, though Sino-American talks are "alike in form" to Soviet-American talks, they are "different in essence." It is necessary to have problems settled with Nixon, temporarily," in part because this will "open up the gate of contacts between the people of China and the United States," but also because the U.S.-China opening "frustrates the strategic deployment of the Soviet revisionists," "aggravates the contradictions between the United States and the Soviet Union," "aggravates the contradictions between US imperialism and its lackeys," "benefits our liberation of Taiwan," and "delays a world war and gains time for us to step up domestic construction and to make good preparations for a world war."

These analyses highlight Mao's distinctive balance-of-power approach to dealing with external threats. The essence of this approach can be summarized, in simplified form, in the following basic principles: (1) The party (and China) should first of all clearly identify the principal enemy at any particular time and then should focus its main efforts on combating that enemy. (2) In confronting this enemy, it should be flexible and exploit all possible contradictions, and it should try to form as broad a united front as feasible, one that will include all who can be induced to oppose the main enemy. (3) In doing this, however, it should maintain a strong posture of self-reliance and should not compromise its essential "independence and initiative." (4) This means that united front "alliances" should be viewed as tactical alignments that are essentially limited and temporary.

This distinctive Maoist approach was first evolved, as already noted, during the Chinese communists' domestic struggle for power, but it was then applied to foreign policy problems, especially in the early 1940s. In the 1970s, it was revived and strongly reemphasized. It represents a conscious effort to apply to foreign policy the kind of flexible united-front strategies that Mao had promoted during China's internal struggles; in a subtle fashion, it also reflects the long-standing Chinese tradition of using "barbarians to oppose barbarians." One can argue that most Chinese leaders during the past century, in attempting to cope with external threats from a position of weakness, have pursued strategies that are comparable in some respects.[15]

The Overall Historical Record

Returning to the fundamental question of the impact of military-security problems, and Chinese communist conceptions of how to best deal with them, on China's overall foreign policy strategies during the past three to four decades, I would argue that to understand Chinese communist foreign policy behavior it is important to keep the following facts (or, if you prefer, propositions) in mind.

(1) For more than thirty years—since well before 1949 (when the Chinese Communist Party was still struggling for power, although it already was, in effect, a "state within a state" and had begun evolving a "foreign policy" of its own)—the Chinese communists' overriding foreign policy preoccupation has been how to deal with the three major powers most deeply involved in Chinese affairs: Japan, the Soviet Union, and the United States. (2) For virtually all of this period, they have seen at least one of these powers as

posing an actual or imminent military threat to China's (and the CCP's) basic security or very survivial. (3) Generally, they have identified one of these powers as posing the main threat (Japan from the 1930s until the mid-1940s, the United States from at least 1950 until the late 1960s and the Soviet Union from the late 1960s on), and they have usually focused their main efforts on the task of deterring or combating that power. (4) Throughout this period, they have been in a position of great military inferiority vis-á-vis the other powers that they have seen as threatening them, and they have been acutely aware of this fact. Their problem there-fore, has been how to deal with militarily superior and actually or potentially threatening powers from a position of relative weakness. (5) Their fundamental approach has been, while building up their own power to the extent they could, to try to strengthen their own position and weaken that of their main enemy by employing united-front-based, balance-of-power strategies and tactics. In doing so, they have been very sensitive to the real military balance; howev-er, they have also placed great emphasis on political and psychological factors in the changing "balance of forces." While their strategies have been essentially defensive in a basic military sense, their policies have often been offensive in a political sense (and, it should be added, have frequently been seen by their adversaries as posing threats to these adversaries' security interests, thereby helping to create situations of tension and conflict that have on many occa-sions increased the apparent threats to China's security.)

Despite the validity, in my view, of the above generaliza-tions, Peking over the years has by no means been consistent, or consistently successful, in applying all of the concepts involved in what might be labeled the "classical Maoist united-front, balance-of-power strategy," as articulated by Mao in 1940. The prescriptions outlined in "On Policy" did shape the Chinese communists' foreign policies in the early 1940s, when the party pursued a very flexible united-front approach in its attempt to mobilize all possible support in the struggle against Japan. New data that have recently come to light on the late 1930s and early 1940s, as well as new studies of Chinese communist foreign policies in that period, indicate, for example, that the party's leaders were prepared to go considerably further than has generally been assumed to try to form a tactical alignment with the United States in order to obtain American military aid.[16]

In the late 1940s, however, Peking's decision to ally with the Soviet Union in order to cope with what the Chinese communist leaders apparently say as a serious potential threat from U.S. power based in Japan (and still linked to the Chinese Nationalists) was consistent with the principles outlined in "On Policy" in some respects, but not in others. For a period of time, especially in the Cold War years just before and during the Korean conflict, Peking (and Moscow as well) adopted a rigid "two-camp" view of the world, which involved a virtual abandonment of the kind of flexibility that Mao had earlier espoused. This began to change from 1952 on, and eventually Peking worked assiduously to build an anti-American united front, periodically changing and steadily broadening its definition of whom to try to include in it. During 1955-1956, at the height of the so-called Bandung period, Chinese policy was extraordinarily flexible; at that time, Peking took various initiatives apparently designed to reduce the level of tension in China's confrontation with the United States, even though the Chinese leadership still regarded Washington as Peking's principal enemy.

In a basic sense, however, the policy of close alliance with the Soviet Union compromised certain important Maoist concepts—or instincts. Instead of maintaining a self-reliant posture, the Chinese communists moved increasingly into a position of dependency on Moscow in the 1950s in ways that seriously weakened China's "independence and initiative." This was, in many respects, an aberration, at least in terms of classical Maoist concepts, and there is little doubt that Mao himself subsequently regarded it as such.

Then, as the Sino-Soviet split widened, China in the 1960s found itself in the worst of all possible worlds, particularly from the Maoist strategic perspective. Instead of confronting only one principal enemy, Peking now faced two (plus India and Japan), and the leadership became increasingly concerned about anti-Chinese collusion between Moscow and Washington. In this situation, with China increasingly isolated, the Chinese leaders put more and more emphasis on the potential importance of Third World nations. However, their efforts to build a united front among these nations against both the superpowers had only limited results in the 1960s; in fact, at the height of the Cultural Revolution, when Peking's leaders turned inward to an extreme degree, China was exceptionally isolated and vulnerable, lacking any effective foreign support to counterbalance the two superpowers, both of which, as Chinese leaders saw it, now posed serious security threats to China.

The dramatic shifts in China's foreign policies between 1968 and 1972 were Peking's response to this situation, and they represented, in many respects, a return to classical Maoist concepts such as those articulated in "On Policy."[17] It was not surprising, therefore, that Mao's earlier writings were resuscitated to justify and explain the far-reaching policy changes, which doubtless surprised most people in China just as much as they surprised people abroad.

Prospects

Looking ahead, should one expect that Peking's current, distinctively Maoist foreign policy strategy will continue to shape China's basic policies for the indefinite future? Should one assume, in short, that Peking will continue to pursue a strategy based on the premise that in the pursuit of its security China should focus its prime efforts on how to deal with one "principal enemy" and, in doing so, should form limited and temporary "alliances" with virtually all enemies of its main enemy? If so, is it likely for the indefinite future to continue to see the Soviet Union as the principal threat, or to continue to believe that loose alignments with countries, such as the United States and Japan, however "limited" or "temporary" it may regard these, are necessary to cope with the Soviet threat? The answer is: possibly but not necessarily.

In foreign as well as domestic affairs, it is risky to assume that there will be unbroken continuity between the Mao and the post-Mao eras.

Certain things do seem probable. For example, it seems highly likely that security problems will continue to be a basic, probably *the* basic, foreign policy preoccupation of Peking's leaders for many years; that, in regard to China's security, Peking's leaders will continue to be concerned above all with China's relations with the three other major powers in East Asia; and that they will continue to view either the Soviet Union or the United States (or both) as the country (or countries) most likely (and able) to pose serious threats to China's security in the foreseeable future (although they are also very much aware of the possibility that if Japan embarks on major rearmament, it could again pose a threat to China). It is also likely that China—because of its military inferiority—will continue to be very vulnerable to threats from the other major powers (especially the two superpowers); that Chinese leaders will continue to be acutely sensitive to this fact; and that to try to compensate for their relative military weakness they will probably continue pursuing a balance-of-power strategy of some sort.

Nevertheless, this does not mean that China's post-Mao leaders will necessarily pursue a "classical Maoist" strategy. It would not be surprising, in fact, if they were to reassess China's foreign policy options. Should they do so, their decisions on basic strategy could be influenced by numerous variables. Here I will mention only three.

One crucial variable will be the kind of post-Mao leadership that emerges in China. There is considerable evidence that in the past some important Chinese leaders have disagreed with Mao's foreign policy strategies. These disagreements have probably focused less on whether China faced actual or potential threats to its security than on how best to cope with such threats. In recent years, for example, some— probably including certain of China's most militant ideologues—appear to have questioned Mao's willingness to compromise with the United States in order to strengthen the alignment of forces opposing the Soviet Union; their inclination seems to have been to oppose compromise with either imperialism or revisionism.[18] Others, probably including some important military leaders, appear to have disagreed with Mao's apparent determination to maintain a posture of hostile confrontation with China's principal enemy while trying to mobilize all possible opposition forces against it.[19] Such people seem periodically to have argued, for example, in favor of a more compromising policy toward Moscow, primarily to reduce the danger of overt military conflict (without necessarily favoring a return to hostile confrontation with the United States). It is quite conceivable that if leaders with this view should come to the fore, there could be a limited Sino-Soviet détente, even though a far-reaching Sino-Soviet rapprochement would still appear highly unlikely.

Future Chinese leaders conceivably could decide, therefore, to move toward a position of even greater flexibility and maneuverability than Mao favored, adopting policies designed to balance all other powers off against each other. If so, they might try to reduce potential threats to China by avoiding direct confrontations with any other power and perhaps even by pursuing policies of cautious, limited détente toward all.

As noted earlier, for a brief period in the mid-1950s, when Chou En-lai's influence on China's foreign policy seemed particularly great, it appeared that Peking might be considering steps in such a direction. It is significant, also, that in the course of defending China's opening to the United States as well as the Maoist confrontation approach to dealing with the Soviet Union, the authors of the Yunnan document cited above revived earlier denunciations of Liu Shao-ch'i for allegedly having promoted a policy of "three reconciliations and one reduction" in the 1960s (meaning, among other things, a policy aimed at improving relations with both the Soviet Union and the United States.) Whatever view one may have of the validity of this accusation,[20] it is plausible that some Chinese leaders have argued for a more compromising approach toward both superpowers, and it is certainly conceivable that if a collective leadership dominated by pragmatic moderates were to emerge, such a leadership could decide to move in that direction.

A second important variable that will clearly influence future strategic options as viewed from Peking will be trends affecting China's actual defensive military capabilities vis-á-vis the two superpowers and Chinese leaders' perceptions of their vulnerability to military threats. If, gradually, over time, Chinese leaders became confident of their ability to deter or counter military threats as the result of an improved military position, the basic arguments for pursuing a classical Maoist balance-of-power strategy could be weakened. In fact, the acquisition by the Chinese of an embryonic nuclear deterrent in the late 1960s and early 1970s may already have had some influence on China's strategic posture, contributing to the Chinese leaders' decision to play down (beginning in late 1973) the dangers of any imminent direct Soviet military threat to China itself while stressing the global Soviet threat, particularly to Europe (although it is difficult to judge to what extent the Chinese really believe their current line on this or are merely promoting it for tactical reasons).

It is not easy, however, to estimate what future trends in China's comparative military position are likely to be or how these are likely to affect the Chinese leaders' sense of military vulnerability. Peking's limited defensive deterrent will probably become increasingly credible in the next few years, but China has no foreseeable prospect of approaching nuclear parity with either the United States or the USSR. In fact, after China has achieved its initial goal of acquiring a minimal deterrent, the gap between China and the superpowers, in terms of total sophisticated nuclear capabilities, conceivably could actually widen. Nor can Chinese leaders be confident that their relative position in conventional military terms will soon improve in any dramatic fashion; in recent years, it has probably deteriorated in some respects as China's aircraft and other items of materiel acquired earlier have become increasingly obsolete. Consequently, even if one assumes that Chinese leaders may acquire a greater sense of confidence in their ability to deter possible nuclear strikes—their overall inferiority in the military balance will doubtless continue. This fact will probably argue in favor of the need to continue pursuing some kind of balance-of-power strategy designed to fend off potential military threats, whether or not this strategy is identical to Mao's.

A third major variable that is certain to affect Peking's overall strategy in the future, as in the past, will be the policies of other major powers toward China. Peking's sense of threat in recent decades has not been without foundation. Even though, as stated earlier, Mao's particular approach to dealing with external threats has tended at times to exacerbate tensions in China's foreign relations in ways that have sometimes increased rather than decreased China's sense of danger, there is no question that both the United States and the Soviet Union, at different times, have pursued policies of containment and pressure directed against China; these have posed threats that have appeared very real from the Chinese perspective and to which Peking has responded with the kind of confrontation-cum-balance-of-power strategies described above.

If in the future a limited Sino-Soviet détente were to occur in parallel with continuing limited détente between the United States and both China and the Soviet Union, one might hope for a break in the action-reaction cycle that has been such a fundamental factor shaping Chinese policies—and those of the other major powers as well—in recent years. However, there is no basis for any confidence that this is likely to happen soon. If it does not, Peking's leaders will probably continue to feel in the period immediately ahead that because China is still relatively weak and vulnerable to potential (even if not imminent) threats, it must pursue some kind of balance-of-power strategy to compensate for its own relative weakness. There remains, however, the question of whether China's post-Mao leaders will choose to continue a classical Maoist balance-of-power strategy or will opt for some new approach, possibly one that calls for more flexibility in dealing with all potentially threatening powers rather than requiring hostile confrontation with one. The answer to that question will help to determine what the prospects are in the period ahead for developing the emerging four-power relationship in East Asia into an equilibrium that will be more stable than the situation that exists today.

The 1958 Quemoy Crisis: The Sino-Soviet Dimension

It is this writer's judgment that the offshore island crisis of 1958 was a critical event that helped to increase the mutual disenchantment between Peking and Moscow and probably had a direct influence on Moscow's decision to cut off nuclear-weapons aid to China—an act that clearly had far-reaching effects on overall Sino-Soviet relations.

Within both the scholarly and the government research communities, there have been different judgments as to the nature of Sino-Soviet relations during the crisis and the effects of the crisis. Some analysts have long maintained that the crisis resulted in serious strains between Peking and Moscow.[21] Others have argued, however, that the Soviets gave the Chinese the kind of support they wanted.[22]

Although it is impossible to find definitive "proof" for any one view, the information now available—including new data that have only recently come to light—strongly supports the thesis that the crisis did contribute significantly to growing Sino-Soviet strains and to the ultimate split.

As is well known, the Chinese have publicly charged that Moscow's statements of support for China on September 7 and 19, 1958, did not come until after "there was no possibility that a nuclear war [with the United States] would break out and no need for the Soviet Union to support China with its nuclear weapons. It was only when they were clear that this was the situation that the Soviet leaders expressed their support for China."[23] Although some analysts have expressed skepticism about the validity of this claim, it seems quite plausible in light of a number of facts that have subsequently emerged.

It now appears very likely, on the basis of statements made by both the Russians and the Chinese, that Mao Tse-tung did not inform Nikita Khrushchev about what China really planned to do regarding the offshore islands, when Khrushchev visited Peking on July 31–August 3, 1958, just before the serious crisis developed. One of Moscow's top government China specialists, M. S. Kapitsa, says that although Chinese plans for action at Quemoy had been made during Khrushchev's stay in Peking, the Chinese "did not consider it necessary to inform him of this."[24] Mao has also indicated that his talks with Khrushchev "did not contain a word about the question of the Taiwan situation."[25]

Some recent Soviet statements directly link the crisis with the problem of nuclear risks and the change in Moscow's nuclear aid policy. In an interview with this writer in Moscow on April 26, 1974, M. S. Kapitsa, the Soviet China specialist just cited, who is chief of the First Far Eastern Department, Ministry of Foreign Affairs, threw new light on the importance of the crisis from the Soviet perspective. He stated the following: in part because Mao had not informed Khrushchev of his specific plans regarding the offshore islands, the Soviet leadership was disturbed when the crisis heated up. To discuss the situation, Foreign Minister A. A. Gromyko made a secret trip to Peking, taking Kapitsa with him.[26] In Peking, Gromyko and Kapitsa met with the Chinese Politburo on September 6. At that meeting, Mao made statements seemingly indicating a relative lack of concern about the dangers of possible nuclear conflict, which the Russians found very disturbing. (The plausibility of Kapitsa's claim is bolstered by the fact that in a speech at a Supreme State Conference on September 5, the day before the Politburo meeting Kapitsa describes, Mao did discuss the nuclear problem and expressed his willingness to take risks regarding possible nuclear attack.[27])

Kapitsa went on to say that shortly after this Moscow reassessed its policy of nuclear-weapons assistance to China, clearly implying a linkage between the crisis and the change in Moscow's policy on nuclear aid. (The Chinese have asserted that on June 20, 1959, the Russians unilaterally "tore up" their October 15,1957, agreement to aid China's nuclear weapons development by providing it with "a sample of an atomic bomb and technical data concerning its manufacture."[28])

Thus, the chronology of certain key events during the critical September 4-7 period apparently was as follows: September 5—Mao's speech to the Supreme State Conference,[29] September 6—the Politburo meeting attended by Gromyko, as described by Kapitsa, and Radio Peking's public broadcast of Chou En-lai's statement at the Supreme State Conference that China was prepared to resume ambassadorial talks with the United States; September 7—Khrushchev's first letter to President Eisenhower supporting China. One plausible hypothesis, based on these data, is that the Chinese and Soviet reactions to U.S. actions were quite different—that Mao seemed, to the Russians, to be too willing to take risks, and that Khrushchev made his September 7 statement of support only *after* the Russians had made clear to the Chinese the limits of Soviet support and induced them to offer to reopen Sino-American negotiations. This hypothesis is not "provable," and there are some facts that seem inconsistent with it. It can be argued, for example, that the real military dangers of the crisis did not recede until after the U.S. Navy had broken the blockade of Quemoy in late September, or perhaps not even until Peking had issued cease-fire orders in October. Moreover, Khrushchev in his memoirs asserts that "we were all in favor of Mao Tse-tung's liquidating these two islands as points for assault" on China and indicated that the Russians were perplexed when the Chinese later told them that Peking had not really wanted to take the islands.[30]

Whether or not one accepts the foregoing hypothesis about events during the period September 4-7, however, the statements made by both the Chinese and Russians convince this writer that there were very serious differences between the two over the crisis, that these increased Sino-Soviet strains significantly, and that they influenced Moscow's decision to cut off Soviet nuclear aid.

Notes

1. This article draws upon research and analysis that the author has done for a book-length study, *China and the Major Powers in East Asia,* which is now completed in draft and is to be published by the Brookings Institution.

2. For a detailed supporting analysis of the 1958 offshore islands crisis—with documentation—see the section titled "The 1958 Quemoy Crisis: The Sino-Soviet Dimension" at the end of this chapter.

3. See, for example, the August 15, 1963, "Statement by the Spokesman of the Chinese Government—A Comment on the Soviet Government Statement of August 3," in *Peking Review,* August 16, 1963, p. 15. This statement said that the Chinese had sent three memorandums to the Soviet government before the signing of the test-ban treaty and declared that Peking had "hoped the Soviet Government would not infringe on China's sovereign rights and act for China in assuming an obligation to refrain from manufacturing nuclear weapons. . . . We hoped that after such earnest counsel from us, the Soviet leaders would rein in before reaching the precipice and would not render matters irretrievable."

4. There is little doubt that the Russians took actions designed to exert pressure on China and eventually to pose the threat of possible attack, and that the Chinese were genuinely fearful of attack at that time. As early as September 1968, Peking charged Moscow with "military provocations over China's air space," asserting that these were "in support of atrocities of aggression against Czechoslovakia." See *Peking Review,* September 20, 1968, p. 41. Soviet nuclear and other threats during 1968 are discussed in the *New York Times,* September 18, 1968, and Harold C. Hinton, *The Bear at the Gate* (Washington, D.C.: American Enterprise Institute and Hoover Institution, 1971), pp. 29-30.

5. See, for example, "Outline of Education on Situation for Companies," translated in *Issues and Studies* (Taipei), June 1974, pp. 90 ff., and July 1974, pp. 99 ff. This document will be discussed in greater detail later.

6. For a brief period during 1970-1971, Peking's propaganda strongly attacked Japanese "militarism," and Chinese leaders at that time may well have actually feared that a decline in the U.S. position in Asia might stimulate Tokyo to rearm on a large scale and move toward assuming a regional military role. Peking quickly dropped this line when openings to the United States and Japan were in the offing.

7. As early as the beginning of 1973, Chou En-lai reportedly told a visiting Japanese official: "Inasmuch as Japan constitutes a nation, weapons of self-defense are essential to it." See the interview with Takeo Kimura, Japan's former Minister of Construction, upon his return from a visit to China, in *Asahi Shimbun* (Tokyo), January 27, 1973. In late 1973, Foreign Minister Chi P'eng-fei reportedly declared that "it is quite natural for Japan to maintain the security treaty with the United States while it lacks sufficient self-defense capacity." See Kyodo News Service, December 17, 1973. By 1975, Chou En-lai was saying: "Japan and the United States should develop even more intimate ties." See "Quarterly Chronicle and Documentation," *The China Quarterly* [London], no. 62 (June 1975), pp. 373-74. Privately, Chinese leaders now assert that U.S.-Japan ties are more important than China-Japan ties.

8. When Kim visited Peking in April 1975, the Chinese declared that they viewed his regime as the "sole legal sovereign state" of Korea and strongly backed his demands for a withdrawal of U.S. forces from South Korea. By this time, the Chinese were no longer telling diplomats of countries other than the United States, as they had earlier, that they were tolerant of U.S. forces in South Korea. However, the Chinese firmly stressed (when Kim was in Peking) the need for "peaceful" reunification, and their

statements were notably less militant than Kim's. See the speeches and communiqué in *Peking Review*, April 25 and May 2, 1975.

9. The strains in Sino-Vietnamese relations were doubtless exacerbated by Chinese seizure of the Paracel Islands, which North Vietnam also claimed.

10. Peking, while endorsing antisubversion statements, did not, however, stop its public encouragement of Southeast Asian communist parties or the radio broadcasts originating in China directed to them, and this continued to disturb noncommunist Southeast Asian governments.

11. See "Quarterly Chronicle and Documentation," *The China Quarterly*, no. 63 (September 1975), pp. 597-600; ibid. no. 63 (December 1975), pp. 809-12.

12. See the text in *Peking Review*, April 12, 1974, Supplement.

13. For the text of "On Policy," see Mao Tse-tung, *Selected Works*, 4 vols. (Peking: Foreign Languages Press, 1965), 2: 441 ff. For the commentary, see "Strong Weapon to Unite the People and Defeat the Enemy—Study 'On Policy'," in Foreign Broadcast Information Service, *Daily Report: People's Republic of China* (Washington, D.C.), August 18, 1971. The following quotations are from this text.

14. See "Outline of Education on Situation for Companies." The following quotations are from this text. There is good reason to accept the authenticity of the document.

15. The Nationalists' policy of alignment with the United States against Japan, while different in many respects, had certain features in common with the Maoist approach.

16. See, especially, U.S. Department of State, *Foreign Relations of the United States, 1944: China* (Washington, D.C.: U.S. Government Printing Office, 1967), and *Foreign Relations of the United States, 1945: China* (Washington, D.C.: U.S. Government Printing Office, 1969). I am grateful also to two scholars for sharing with me their still-unpublished drafts of two excellent studies on the period: Steven Goldstein, *The View From Yenan: Chinese Commu-*

nist Perspectives on International Relations, 1937-1941, and James Reardon-Anderson, *Yenan: The Foreign Policy of Self-Reliance.*

17. Goldstein, *The View from Yenan*, also points this out.

18. The quotation cited earlier about "some comrades" who "slander and vilify" the policy of opening contacts with Washington (taken from "Outline of Education on Situation for Companies") is very revealing about existing doubts concerning, and opposition to, compromise with the United States; various kinds of circumstantial evidence suggest that such opposition came especially from ideological leftists, who have also criticized increased economic intercourse and—even more so—expanded cultural contacts with Western nations. In 1974, such attacks focused on a "slavish" mentality about foreign things and on being servile lackeys of imperialism who "view foreigners as one hundred percent perfect and ourselves as totally incompetent." See, as examples, articles in *Peking Review*, February 1, 1974, pp. 7-10, and in *Selections from People's Republic of China Magazines* (Hong Kong), September 20, 1974, pp. 1-3.

19. The following are examples of recent articles that indicate continuing debate on whether to pursue a confrontation policy or a more compromising policy toward the Soviet Union: "Lo Ssu-ting Discusses Patriotism, National Betrayal," *Hung Ch'i* (Red Flag—Peking), no. 11, 1974, in Foreign Broadcast Information Service, *Daily Report: People's Republic of China*, November 20, 1974, pp. E1-10, and An Miao, "Confucianist Capitulationism and Traitor Lin Piao," *Jen-min Jih-pao* (People's Daily—Peking), August 12, 1975, in *Survey of People's Republic of China Press* (Hong Kong), August 22, 1975, pp. 171-80.

20. Liu Shao-ch'i himself implied at one point that Teng Hsiao-p'ing had proposed such a policy, but Liu later claimed that he had not known about it. See *Collected Works of Liu Shao-ch'i, 1958-1967* (Hong Kong: Union Research Institute, 1968), pp. 361 and 367). Even if Liu did not promote this line, it is highly likely, in light of the charges

made, that some important leader(s) did.

21. See, for example, Donald S. Zagoria, *The Sino-Soviet Conflict, 1956-61* (Princeton, N.J.: Princeton University Press, 1967), pp. 206-16, and John R. Thomas, "The Limits of Alliance: The Quemoy Crisis of 1958," in *Sino-Soviet Military Relations*, ed. Raymond L. Garthoff (New York: Praeger, 1966), pp. 114-49.

22. See, for example, Morton H. Halperin, *China and the Bomb* (New York: Praeger, 1965), p. 55, footnote 46.

23. See "Statement by the Spokesman of the Chinese Government," September 1, 1963; text in Garthoff, *Sino-Soviet Military Relations*, pp. 233 ff.

24. See M. S. Kapitsa, *Communist China—Two Decades—Two Policies* (Moscow: The Political Literature Publishing House, 1969), trans. in Joint Publications Research Service, *Reports* (Washington, D.C.), no. 51425, September 22, 1971, p. 194.

25. See Allen S. Whiting, "New Light on Mao—3. Quemoy 1958: Mao's Miscalculations," *The China Quarterly* (London), June 1975, p. 269, quoting from a speech by Mao on November 30, 1958, unpublished at the time in China but contained in *Mao Tse-tung Ssu-hsiang Wan-sui* [Long Live Mao Tse-tung's Thought], n.p., August 1969, p. 254.

26. This trip has never been explicitly mentioned in public print, as far as I know, although Kapitsa, on p. 194 of his book, refers in passing to a talk between Gromyko and Mao "in the beginning of September 1958."

27. See the extracts of the speech—taken from the text in *Mao Tse-tung Ssu-hsiang Wan-sui*, 1969, pp. 236-37—which are quoted in Whiting, "New Light on Mao," p. 268.

28. See the August 15, 1963, "Statement by the Spokesman of the Chinese Government—A Comment on the Soviet Government Statement of August 3," *Peking Review*, August 16, 1963, p. 14.

29. See note 25. Mao, Chou En-lai, and others made additional speeches to the Supreme State Conference, which met September 5-9.

30. See *Khrushchev Remembers: The Last Testament,* trans. and ed. Strobe Talbott (Boston: Little, Brown and Co., 1974), pp. 262-63.

4. The Soviet Union and the Far East

Donald S. Zagoria

Despite a massive increase of its military power in Asia during recent years, the Soviet Union has been unable so far to project its power and influence in the region. Nowhere in the Far East has the Soviet Union secured any genuine allies. Relations with all of the major powers in Asia are strained or troubled. Moscow's cold war with China continues even after the death of Mao. Soviet relations with Japan are troubled by continued disputes over fishing rights, territorial issues, and Japan's flirtation with China. Soviet relations with India now seem to be entering a more difficult phase after the defeat of Indira Gandhi and the emergence of a new government determined to improve relations with Washington. Soviet relations with Indonesia have been distant ever since the overthrow of Sukarno. Soviet relations with Australia are deteriorating since the new conservative government has taken to sounding a public alarm about the spread of Soviet naval power in the Pacific. Even in its relations with the smaller communist states of Asia, Moscow can find little room for satisfaction. North Korea is more of an embarrassment than an asset; both Vietnam and Laos are moving to improve relations with Washington in order to obtain economic assistance; and Cambodia is oriented towards Peking.

In the essay that follows, I want to look closely at Soviet relations with several selected Asian countries in an effort to determine why Soviet fortunes in Asia are so low. I will examine in some detail Moscow's relations with China, Japan, and North Korea. I will look more cursorily at Soviet relations elsewhere in Asia. Finally, I will try to offer some general explanations for the lack of Soviet success.

The Bear and The Dragon: Continued Tension

The Causes of Conflict

In retrospect, it can be seen that the Sino-Soviet alliance of 1950 was an artificial alliance. The huge cultural and psychological gap between China and Russia made it impossible for the two countries to achieve any real degree of intimacy. Russia had its cultural heritage in Europe and in Christianity. No cultural tradition could be further removed from that of the Chinese, who developed in splendid isolation from Europe for more than 2,000 years. Russia has deep historical memories of invasion by Mongols and Crimean Tatars, and this has reinforced its racial fears of the "yellow peril." As for China, the intensity of modern Chinese nationalism, reacting against a century of humiliation at the hands of Europe, makes it difficult for any Chinese government to enter into a close relationship with any white, European power, particularly one such as Russia, which participated in the territorial expansion of the nineteenth century at China's expense.

Geopolitics also plays an important role in the Sino-Soviet conflict. The record of Russian-Chinese relations from the seventeenth century on was one of mounting Russian pressure against a weakening Manchu empire in the struggle over the borderlands.[1] As that expansion gained momentum in the middle of the nineteenth century, it led to the imposition of a series of treaties on China that confirmed the Russian seizure of vast amounts of Chinese territories in the Far East, on the Mongolian plateau, and in the steppe lands of inner Asia.

Even the accession to power in both countries of communist parties supposedly devoted to internationalist principles did not put an end to geopolitical rivalry over the borderlands. Within a few years after coming to power in Russia, the Bolsheviks quickly detached Outer Mongolia from the young Chinese republic and set it up as a satellite state. At the same time, they reasserted their influence in northern Manchuria and Sinkiang. At Yalta in 1945, Stalin's major demands for entering the Pacific war against Japan were territorial demands having to do with Outer Mongolia, Manchuria, Sakhalin, and the Kurile Islands. And when Stalin signed the pact with Mao in 1950, he continued to insist on Russian rights in the borderlands.

On the Chinese side, there were equally intense concerns over the borderlands, even after the Sino-Soviet alliance came into being. In 1954, within a year of Stalin's death, Mao purged Manchurian communist leader Kao Kang for seeking to develop an "independent kingdom" that had too intimate relations with Moscow. In the same year, Mao raised with Khrushchev the question of the status of Outer Mongolia and received a cold rebuff. In 1957, at a time when Sino-Soviet relations were outwardly warm, Chou En-lai once again raised territorial questions with Khrushchev but could not get a satisfactory response.

This incipient rivalry over the borderlands in the 1950s became much more serious in the mid-1960s, when Russia began a massive military buildup on the Chinese frontier.[2] Between 1965 and 1972, the number of Soviet ground forces on the Chinese border more than tripled, Soviet tactical air strength grew five times, and the Soviet Pacific Fleet was expanded and modernized.[3] As of now, there are forty-five Soviet divisions facing China, and they are supported by about 200 IRBMs, most of them SS-4 missiles carrying twenty-five megaton warheads, and 1,200 to 1,400 aircraft, including the Backfire bomber, which has a nuclear capability.[4] The Russians have also signed a defense agreement with Outer Mongolia, which is only 450 miles from Peking, that allows them to station troops and maintain bases in that country. Soviet tank and missile units are now occupying permanent bases there.

The rivalry between the two Eurasian empires is, moreover, intensified by the fact that most of the inhabitants of the vast border areas between the two countries are peoples of minority nationalities whose loyalty to the regimes in power in Moscow and Peking cannot be taken for granted. And, in the history of both countries, the border areas, which have no natural defense barriers, have proven to be invasion routes. China's rich Yangtse River valley has traditionally been the target of invaders from the north, and Russia's Far Eastern territories, far removed from European Russia, were invaded by the Western powers and Japan during the Civil War and were the object of Japanese incursions in the late 1930s.

In addition to the cultural and geopolitical gap between Russia and China, there are also substantial differences of national interest. It was not in Russia's interests to help China become a major nuclear power, and the alliance floundered when Khrushchev began to renege on his promise of helping China to develop nuclear weapons. Nor was it in China's interests to become so dependent on Russia. Mao would have preferred to maneuver between Moscow and Washington from the moment he took power in 1949, but the American policy of nonrecognition gave China little alternative to lopsided dependence on Russia.[5] Now that both Russia and China have serious internal economic problems, it is in the interests of both countries to cultivate closer relations with the United States, Japan, and Western Europe, countries that can supply sorely needed economic and technological assistance.

These differences of national interest are also reflected in growing competition between the two great powers for influence, particularly in Africa and Asia. This competition is particularly intense in areas where American power is weak or receding, as in southern Africa and Southeast Asia.

Finally, ideology has been *both* a unifying and a divisive element in Sino-Soviet relations, as it has been in church history. A common scriptural inheritance provides a certain unity of outlook, but differing interpretations of the same scripture in accordance with different national needs provide the raw material for conflict. Moreover, once differences of interest are elevated to differences over ideological principles, they are much more difficult to compromise. Once the ideological conflict erupts into an open break, the threat to each side in the controversy becomes extremely serious because the very basis of regime legitimacy is challenged by a rival interpretation of the faith. That is why heretics have always been more dangerous than pagans.

Although the Sino-Soviet conflict does therefore seem to be rooted in several enduring realities of culture, race, nationalism, geopolitics, divergent national interests, and ideology, the conflict has been accelerated and deepened by Soviet overreactions to the Chinese "threat." It is certain that the Soviet forces on the Chinese border now possess a capability far in excess of what would be required to stop a Chinese attack. The massive Soviet buildup on the Chinese frontier was either an overreaction to the Chinese threat or a political blunder intended to cow the Chinese into accommodation. But whatever its motivation, the Soviet buildup so close to the Chinese border has driven Peking into the arms of the United States, has made much more difficult any possibility of a Sino-Soviet accommodation, and has convinced many countries, in addition to China, that the Soviet Union has expansionist aims.

This particular overreaction, moreover, fits the general pattern of Soviet behavior towards China in recent years. The abrupt Soviet withdrawal of its technicians and assistance to China in the early 1960s was another example of crude pressure tactics that proved to be counterproductive. Later, the ill-conceived Soviet plan for an Asian collective security pact was seen by most Asian countries, including China, as a thinly disguised device to encircle China, and it therefore never got off the ground. More recently, the Russians have greatly stepped up the pace of their diplomatic, economic, and intelligence activities throughout Southeast Asia in another crude effort to "contain" China in an area that cannot be of vital interest to Moscow.

In sum, Soviet policy towards China during the past two decades has been a policy of overreaction. The Russians have been short on patience and long on pressure tactics. Their strategy of surrounding China with hostile alliances, reminiscent of the American strategy in the 1950s, has given Peking few alternatives but to enter into a more cooperative relationship with the United States and Japan.

The great irony of the postwar era is that it was in the United States, not in Russia, that the great debate over "who lost China?" took place. But China was never America's to lose. It was Russia's loss, and it was almost certainly the most significant Russian loss of the entire postwar era.

Continued Stalemate in Sino-Soviet Relations Since the Death of Mao

During the past two years, there has been little indication of any improvement in Sino-Soviet relations. The new Chinese Premier, Hua Kuo-feng, in his first speech as acting premier in February 1976, while Mao was still alive, fiercely attacked the Soviet Union in the presence of former President Nixon for expansionism and aggression. When Hua was named Premier in April 1976, he stepped up his attacks on the Soviet Union, using such words as "criminal plans," "subversion," and "sabotage" to describe Soviet policies in Egypt.

Since the death of Mao in September 1976, the intensity of Chinese polemics against the Soviet Union has not subsided. A casual review of the Chinese press between October 1976 and April 1977 is instructive. In October, the Russians were accused of armed occupation of Czechoslovakia, military provocation against China, suppression of the Polish workers' uprising, tightening their grip on Eastern Europe, dismemberment of Pakistan, and armed intervention in Angola.[6] In November, the Russians were charged with intruding on Japan's air space, imperiling the livelihood of Japanese fishermen, engineering a war in southern Africa, trying to force Egypt into submission, seeking new footholds in Latin America, casting a covetous eye on Oceania, and pursuing a blatant gunboat policy in the oceans of the world.[7] In December, Moscow's military deployments against Western Europe were described by the Chinese in loving detail. The Russians, according to Peking, were seeking to bring crude pressure on the whole of Western Europe, but particularly on Norway and Denmark in order to dominate the Baltic approaches to the Atlantic.[8] In January 1977, Peking accused Moscow of practicing a "détente fraud" by which it sought to veil its object of world domination.[9] In February, the Russians were charged with using their trading activities in Southeast Asia as a cover for espionage and for exploiting the East European countries by raising the price of oil.[10] And in March, the Russians were accused of exploiting and oppressing the non-Russian peoples in Soviet Central Asia.[11]

By February 1977, the Russians, who had declared a moratorium on all polemics with Peking immediately after the death of Mao, had once again begun to attack the Chinese, although still in a relatively subdued manner, for inventing anti-Soviet fabrications and making unfriendly statements that poisoned the relations between the two countries.[12]

Although the on again–off again border talks resumed after Mao's death, they were quickly suspended, and a recent Chinese press article claims that the Soviet side has "refused to keep its promises," an apparent allusion to Kosygin's pledge in 1969 to remove Soviet troops from disputed areas.[13]

The Chinese leaders have also spurned several Soviet moves aimed at reconciliation. They returned a message of condolence from the CPSU after Mao's death on the grounds that party-to-party relations did not exist, and there have been reports that Rumanian President Ceausescu's attempts to mediate the dispute have shown no result.[14]

At the same time, Peking appears to be sending signals to Washington that there will be no accommodation with Moscow and that differences with the United States over Taiwan should not obstruct the common objectives that

Washington and Peking have in containing Soviet power. On January 28, 1977, a long article prepared by the Chinese Ministry of Foreign Affairs noted pointedly that Chairman Mao had always placed "great hopes in the American people" and went on to observe that the Chinese government had always stood for a settlement of the Taiwan question through negotiations without resorting to force.

It is noteworthy, too, that the campaign against the "gang of four" inside China has recently been expanded to include charges that those errant Chinese leaders were "soft" on the Soviet Union, a sure indication that no change of line on relations with Moscow is intended in the near future.

What are we to make of this continued anti-Soviet line from Peking and this continued "tilt"toward the United States? Will it last? Or will Peking, at some point in the future, seek to reduce tensions with Moscow in order to play the triangular balance of power more effectively as many observers have predicted?

As has often been observed by this author as well as others,[15] the Chinese should have some powerful interests in reducing tensions with the Russians. Normalization with Moscow might diminish Soviet pressure on the border, reduce Chinese defense burdens at a time when economic growth—particularly in agriculture—is lagging, and enable China to exercise more leverage on the United States over such outstanding issues as Taiwan. On the other hand, it is increasingly problematic whether Moscow is prepared to make the kinds of concessions on the border that Peking insists upon—substantial troop withdrawals from contested areas. (Recent Soviet visitors to the United States have argued that large Soviet forces on the Chinese border are necessary to protect the trans-Siberian railroad, which, at some points, runs only 50 to 100 kilometers from the border.) The Chinese may calculate that they can cut defense burdens somewhat even without giving in to Moscow on the grounds that the Russians are already deterred from massive military intervention into China. And while China might obtain more leverage over the United States by normalizing relations with Russia, it also stands to lose a good deal from such an accommodation.

Let me list some of the things that China might lose from an accommodation with Moscow. First, Sino-Soviet accommodation, even a limited accommodation, might frighten both the United States and Japan at a time when China needs trade and technology from the West in order to modernize. According to Dernberger's calculations, China's economic growth over the next fifteen years is dependent upon "significant imports of food grains, producer's goods (and technology), chemical fertilizers and metals."[16] These goods can only be obtained from the industrialized and agricultural-surplus nations in the West and from Japan. The Soviet Union and Eastern Europe simply cannot supply the imports that China needs. Thus, China's economic growth over the next fifteen years will depend to a considerable extent on maintaining stable trade relations with the Western world.

Moreover, at some point, China may well want long term and large-scale credits from the West in order to finance larger imports. If China were to normalize relations with Moscow, particularly at a time when the United States is visibly concerned with the Soviet military buildup, it would be much more difficult for any American administration to step up trade with China.

A Sino-Soviet accommodation would also make it difficult for the United States to make even the slightest concession to the Chinese on the issue of Taiwan. One of the principal arguments now being made for U.S. concessions on Taiwan is that unless Sino-American relations are improved, there will be an increasing chance of a Sino-Soviet accommodation. This argument would be bankrupt were such an accommodation actually to take place.

Third, a Sino-Soviet accommodation might encourage the United States and Japan to speed up the pace of normalizing their own relations with Moscow and thus leave Peking with few cards to play against the Russians. Fourth, whatever new leadership finally emerges in Peking will

require legitimation on the basis of accepted Maoist principles, particularly the notion that China represents true,
unperverted socialism. Any accommodation with Moscow
might appear as a radical break with the Maoist legacy and
thus deprive the new leadership of an important element of
legitimacy.

But there is a final and perhaps even more powerful reason
why Peking may have more to lose than to gain from an
accommodation with Moscow. There can be no doubt that
the Soviet Union is determined over the next decade or two to
become a major Pacific power. The rise of the Soviet Union
as a Pacific power will be dictated by several considerations.
First, Moscow is determined to match the United States as a
global power capable of deploying its forces anywhere in the
world, including the Pacific Basin. Second, the post-
Vietnam decline of American power in the Pacific, the
continuing military weakness of Japan, and the extraordinary Soviet fear of a future Pacific combination involving
American, Japanese, and Chinese power will ensure a steady
Soviet buildup of its naval power in the Pacific as well as
continuing efforts through political and other means to
expand Soviet influence throughout the Far East. Finally,
the steady development of the huge untapped mineral and
other natural resources in Siberia and the Soviet Far East—
one third of all investment in the current Soviet Five-Year
Plan is devoted to the Asian regions of Russia—will mean
that within the next two decades the Soviet Union will
emerge as a major economic—as well as military— power in
the Pacific. In the light of these considerations, Moscow will
be increasingly unwilling to remove its forces from the
Chinese border. Already the military geography of the Sino-
Soviet border has been permanently altered by the establishment of missile depots, underground tunnels, and storage
bases all along the frontier. This rise of Soviet power in the
Pacific is not, in sum, a short-range phenomenon dictated by
tactical consideration. It seems to be a permanent feature of
Soviet policy, and it will present China over the long run
with only two real alternatives—either to accommodate to

Soviet power or to seek to balance it. Because the Soviet Union is not likely to offer accommodation on easy terms, and because the Chinese are fiercely nationalistic and profoundly suspicious of Soviet intentions, China is much more likely to opt for the second alternative.

Two other considerations need to be added to this assessment. First, in both China and in Russia, the military is now playing a larger role than ever before. The result of this ascendancy of the military is likely to be that strategic, rather than ideological, considerations will become increasingly paramount in the calculations of both leaderships. On balance, this is likely to make accommodation more difficult. While it is possible, as some observers have suggested, that there are elements in the Chinese military who want to normalize relations with Moscow in order to reduce tensions on the border, it is equally likely that other elements in the Chinese military want to raise defense spending in order to modernize the badly outdated Chinese armed forces and that they find the Soviet "menace" a convenient pretext to argue for such increases. Soviet generals are also likely to find the Chinese "threat" a good rationale for higher defense budgets. Indeed, I have heard on good authority that in 1969 the Soviet marshals were instrumental in blocking the border agreement that had been virtually concluded between Chou En-lai and Kosygin.

Second, the competition between the two powers for influence in Africa and Asia is likely to grow even more sharply in the period ahead. Thus, in the foreseeable future, even a limited accommodation between Russia and China seems unlikely. Even if such an accommodation were to occur, it is likely to prove highly unstable.

The Soviet Union and Japan: Troubled Waters

Soviet relations with Japan can be divided into five major policy issues: the peace treaty, the territorial dispute, fishing rights, Siberian development, and the problem of security, which involves China and the United States as well as the Soviet Union and Japan.

In four of these five areas, relations between Moscow and Tokyo are strained. Thirty-two years after the end of World War II, there still is no peace treaty between the two countries. The major obstacle to the conclusion of such a treaty is the territorial dispute over four of the Kurile Islands now occupied by Moscow but claimed by Tokyo. There is virtually no chance of this issue being resolved in the foreseeable future. Fishing rights are a perennial problem between the two countries, and they are likely to get worse as a result of Moscow's recent declaration of a 200-mile exclusive fishing zone. On security issues, Moscow looks with growing alarm at the Japanese détente with China and the Japanese security relationship with the United States, a combination that could ultimately lead to a Chinese-American-Japanese entente. Tokyo, on the other hand, is increasingly uneasy about the growth of the Soviet Pacific Fleet. Only in the area of Siberian development and trade is there a relatively bright spot in Soviet-Japanese relations. Soviet trade with Japan has been growing steadily since the 1960s, and Japan has provided more than a billion dollars in credits to several Siberian projects involving the development of coal, oil, natural gas, and timber. Still, the volume of these credits falls far short of Soviet expectations.

Underlying the difficulties over many of these issues is substantial mutual mistrust and suspicion stemming from a modern history of conflict. The Russians still recall their humiliating defeat at the hands of the Japanese in 1905, the Japanese intervention in Siberia in the 1920s, and the border wars of 1937-1939, when Japan was intent on dominating Manchuria. The Japanese still recall Moscow's unilateral abrogation of the Neutrality Pact in order to join in the kill in the last eight days of World War II. The Russians captured half a million Japanese soldiers in Manchuria and kept them in concentration camps for ten years.

The MIG-25 Incident

In September 1976, a new irritant was added to the Soviet Japanese relationship when a Soviet pilot landed a MIG-25

in Hakodate and sought asylum in the United States. After
some initial hesitation, the Japanese decided to retain the
aircraft, which was believed to be extremely sophisticated, in
order to inspect it. Japan also decided to cooperate with the
United States in dismantling and examining the aircraft
before shipping it back to the Soviet Union. This incident
brought the latent Soviet-Japanese suspicions to the surface.
Soviet General Secretary Brezhnev declared that Japan had
"destroyed friendly relations between the two countries," the
Soviet Ambassador to the UN gave his Japanese counterpart
very cold treatment at a meeting in late September 1976, and
the Russians stepped up their harassment of Japanese
fishermen in the waters off Japan, especially near the disputed islands, while postponing a Soviet-Japanese Economic
Committee meeting scheduled for October 1976.

The Peace Treaty and the Territorial Dispute

The most recent discussions on the peace treaty took place
in January 1976, when Soviet Foreign Minister Gromyko
visited Tokyo. These discussions revealed continuing rigidi-
ty on both sides over the main obstacle to a peace treaty,
namely, the dispute over four of the Kurile Islands.

The Kurile Islands are a 1200-km chain of thirty-six
islands linking Japan's northernmost island of Hokkaido
with the Soviet Kamchatka Peninsula. Russia now occupies
all of the Kurile Islands, and Japan claims the four southern-
most islands, closest to Hokkaido. These four include Hokkaido's two offshore islands, Shikotan and Habomai (which
is actually a group of very small islands), and the two larger
islands immediately northeast of Hokkaido, Kunashiri and
Etorofu. The Soviet claims are based on Yalta agreements
concluded during World War II, which the Japanese say are
not binding because they were signed without Japan's
participation or knowledge. At Yalta, Franklin Roosevelt,
acting on the mistaken assumption that Japan had seized the
Kuriles from Russia in 1905, awarded all of the islands to
Russia. He did not read a State Department memorandum
recommending that Japan retain the southern Kuriles to

which they had historic claims. It took only five minutes for FDR to dispose of the islands in a fifteen minute session with Stalin.[17]

The Soviet position on the four southern islands has remained intransigent. Soviet spokesmen say the territorial question is "settled." For a period in the mid-1950s, Soviet leaders did offer to return the two smaller offshore islands to Japan in exchange for a peace treaty, but in more recent years Moscow has seemed to balk even at such a gesture.

There are probably several reasons for Soviet intransigence on the island issue. First, there is a deep (and perhaps obsessive) historically rooted Soviet concern for frontier security. Acting on this concern during World War II, Stalin redrew almost all of the Soviet Union's frontiers. In Europe, he annexed eastern Poland, Bessarabia, and northern Bukovina, all three of the Baltic states of Latvia, Lithuania, and Estonia, and he redrew the Karelian Isthmus boundary with Finland. In the Far East, Stalin annexed southern Sakhalin, which had been under Japanese sovereignty after Japan defeated Russia in 1905, and the four southern Kurile Islands, which had all historically been part of Japan. Indeed, Stalin's major demands, first with the Nazis during the Soviet-German Pact period and later with the victorious allies, were territorial demands.

Moscow's concern for frontier security is intensified by the fact that most of its frontier areas are inhabited by non-Russians. In the Far East, the frontier security problem is exacerbated by the sparse population of the areas, their great distance from European Russia, and their proximity to three hostile powers, China, Japan, and the United States.

The second reason for Soviet intransigence on the Kurile Island issue is the strategic importance of the islands. A glance at the map will demonstrate this. The Kurile Islands arc constitutes a screen along the Northeast Asian littoral. It guards the maritime approaches to the Soviet Far East, provides a gateway to Kamchatka, and guarantees Soviet access to the Pacific. Since 1945, Russia has used the Kurile chain to turn the Sea of Okhotsk into a Soviet lake and to project growing Soviet naval power into the Pacific. The two larger southern islands, Kunashiri and Etorofu, are studded with air bases for reconnoitering Japan's Pacific littoral and for monitoring air traffic between Japan and North America.[18]

A third reason for Soviet intransigence on the island issue is the importance of the Kuriles to the Soviet fishing industry. Far Eastern waters account for about one-third of the total Soviet catch.

Finally, any softening of the Soviet stand on the Kurile issue would open up a "Pandora's box" of territorial issues from World War II. Poland, Rumania, the Baltic republics, Finland, as well as Japan, might be encouraged to reopen territorial questions. Soviet softness on the territorial issue with Japan might also encourage the Chinese to take a much tougher stand on their unresolved territorial questions with the Russians.

But if Moscow is intransigent on the territorial question, so is Tokyo. Nationalistic sentiment on the islands runs high in Japan. The mass media, public opinion polls, and all the political parties support the Japanese government's position. Indeed, many of the opposition parties, including several on the left, want the entire Kurile arc returned to Japan following the conclusion of a peace treaty. Public opinion polls show that one-third of the Japanese populace supports this demand for the return of all the islands. In addition, a sizable portion of the Japanese public wants Russia to return southern Sakhalin to Japan as well. Given this intransigence on both sides, a compromise seems unlikely.

Fishing Disputes

Disputes over fishing rights have also been a continuing irritant in the Soviet-Japanese relationship. This problem may well become worse. As pollution poisons more marine life in Japan's own coastal waters, Japanese fishermen are forced to range into waters further removed from their own coast. Yet the Soviet Union has now declared a 200-mile

exclusive fishing zone, which would severely limit Japanese
fishing rights. There will be no immediate impact on the
Japanese fishing industry because the present fishing agreement continues through 1977. But if the Russians take a very
tough position on a new fishing agreement, this could
further aggravate relations. Moreover, during the past
twenty-five years more than 1300 Japanese fishing boats
have been captured by the Russians; many of these boats
have not been released and substantial numbers of Japanese
fishermen are still held in Russian prisons.

Security Problems and the Sino-Soviet Dispute

From a strategic point of view, both Moscow and Tokyo
have cause for concern about the future intentions of the
other side. The Russians look with alarm at the growing
signs of military coordination between Tokyo and Washington and the occasional signs that Tokyo may tilt toward
Peking in the Sino-Soviet conflict. For Moscow this raises
the specter of a U.S.-Japanese-Chinese alliance. So concerned are the Russians at this prospect that they have put a
great deal of pressure on the Japanese not to sign a peace
treaty with China that contains a key "anti-hegemony"
clause, which is implicitly directed against the Russians.
When Gromyko visited Tokyo in January 1976, he warned
that if Japan were to sign such a treaty, Moscow would
reconsider its whole relationship with Japan. Moscow is
equally concerned about signs of growing Japanese military
power and Japanese-American military cooperation. It was
this concern that produced such an intense Soviet response
to the MIG-25 incident.

Japan, for its part, is concerned about the expansion of
Soviet naval power in the Pacific. Before World War II, the
Pacific waters were divided between the American and
Japanese navies. In the immediate postwar period, the U.S.
Navy had unchallenged dominance of the Pacific. Now the
Soviet Union is challenging that American naval domi-
nance and, in the process, is casting its shadow on the
countries bordering the Pacific Ocean.

The Soviet Navy sent its first aircraft carrier to sea in 1976, and six such carriers are projected. The Soviet submarine fleet is already the largest in the world. The class of missile-armed destroyers is being expanded. The role of the Soviet Naval Air Force seems to be growing.[19]

During worldwide naval exercises in 1975, Soviet naval activity extended throughout the entire Pacific. In just the past few years, the Soviets have extended their naval presence to the East China Sea and to the Yellow Sea. Although traditionally the military modernization of Soviet forces in the east has lagged behind the modernization of Soviet forces in the west, this lag is now being eliminated. MIG-23s, MIG-15s, and SU-19s are now being deployed on the eastern front. In recent years, too, Soviet intelligence ships have approached Japanese shores and ships very closely, and these activities have become a subject of considerable concern in Japanese defense circles.

Siberian Development and Economic Relations

The one potentially bright spot for Soviet-Japanese relations lies in the common interest that both countries have in the development of Siberian natural resources. Moscow has at least two urgent reasons for wanting to develop the Soviet Far East rapidly. First, it needs the gas, oil, coal, and metals of Siberia for its own economic development and for the development of an East European empire that is rapidly becoming a burden. Second, because of its long-range fear of China, the Soviet Union is intent on developing Siberia and increasing its population.

Japan is crucial to Soviet development plans for Siberia for at least two reasons. First, Moscow does not have the necessary capital or technology to develop Siberia on its own. Second, Japan is a natural trading partner for the Soviet Far East because it is so close.

The Japanese, for their part, are almost totally dependent on imports of industrial raw materials, fuel, foodstuffs, and semifinished products which amount to more than 80 percent of their imports. By helping to develop Siberian resources, Japan could gain access to these resources.

These common interests in developing Siberia have already led to more than a billion dollars worth of Japanese investment in various Siberian projects. These include the joint development of coking coal deposits in south Yakutia, exploration for natural gas in Yakutsk, joint exploration for oil and natural gas on the continental shelf of Sakhalin, and development of Siberian timber.

Still, while Japanese investment in the development of Siberian resources is likely to continue, it is likely to proceed at a very deliberate pace. For obvious reasons, the Japanese do not have an interest in helping to develop Soviet military power in the Far East. Since 1974, when the Russians decided to build a second trans-Siberian railroad from Lake Baikal to the Amur, a railroad that could be used for military as well as for economic purposes, the Japanese interest in helping to develop Tyumen oil has virtually ended. This project was to have involved at least a billion dollars in Japanese credits.

Second, since the first Japanese-Chinese oil agreement of January 1973, the Japanese have seemed to be in less of a hurry to help develop Siberian resources, and they have also seemed to harden their position on the Kurile Island issue. Thus, Tokyo's "China card" gives it some additional leverage against the Russians. Third, there is a strong fear in Japan of becoming overly dependent on Russian energy. Fourth, the dearth of technical data from the Soviet side concerning the exact amounts and precise locations of energy resources has increased Japanese suspicions that Soviet claims cannot be taken at face value. Finally, the Japanese are unlikely to enter into any huge deals with the Russians unless they can get the United States to enter with them on a joint basis.

Thus, although Japanese-Soviet cooperation in developing Siberian resources can be expected to continue, it is likely to develop at a much slower pace than the Russians had originally anticipated, and it is unlikely that Moscow will reap the kinds of political benefits that it expected—a shelving by the Japanese of the territorial question and a loosening of Japanese ties to the United States and China.

In sum, the Soviet-Japanese relationship is filled with mutual suspicions, fears, and conflicts of national interest that are not likely to be resolved in the foreseeable future. The Russians have not demonstrated much flexibility in their dealings with Japan. They failed to take advantage of the opportunities created by the "Nixon shock" to Japan in 1972, when the United States entered into a dialogue with China without first informing the Japanese. They seem to have greatly overestimated Japan's need for Siberian resources and to have greatly underestimated the intensity of the Japanese feeling over the territorial question. Most important, Moscow has robbed itself of flexibility on the territorial question by taking such a narrow view of its own frontier security requirements. Although there can be no doubt that Moscow has genuine strategic concerns in the Kurile Island arc, there is room for doubt whether it requires control over all of the islands to guarantee its security.

Moscow and Pyongyang: The Strained Alliance*

Although Moscow and Pyongyang have a mutual defense treaty, a common ideology, and extensive economic and military relations, the relationship between the two communist powers has been troubled ever since the late 1950s, when the North Korean dictator, Kim Il Sung, after a series of purges, was able to assert his leadership against a series of leaders whom Kim subsequently accused of trying to subvert him with Russian assistance.[20] By 1958, Kim, who had been installed in power by Russian troops during the Soviet occupation of the northern part of Korea at the end of World War II, had created an independent power base, overcome the remnants of internal opposition, and asserted his independence from both Moscow and Peking.

The Sino-Soviet split, which emerged in the 1950s, greatly strengthened Kim's ability to maintain his independence by

*This section is a revised version of my article in *Chinese Affairs*, The Institute for China Studies, Hanyang University, Seoul, Korea, 1977.

allowing him to play off the Russians against the Chinese, a game at which he has been particularly proficient ever since.

Since the early 1960s, Soviet relations with North Korea have moved through several stages. Between 1962 and 1964, when Soviet Premier Khrushchev was determined to read China out of the communist bloc and unwilling to tolerate any waverers on the issue, Kim tilted toward Peking. By 1964, the year of Khrushchev's ouster, relations between Moscow and Pyongyang had deteriorated to a point where North Korea publicly accused the Russians of "big-power chauvinism," "xenophobia," and exploitation.[21]

Immediately after Khrushchev's ouster, relations between Moscow and Pyongyang began to improve rapidly. One month after the ouster of Khrushchev, a North Korean Politburo member attended the November 1964 anniversary in Moscow of the 1917 Revolution—the first high-ranking North Korean leader to visit Moscow in three years. This gesture was followed by Premier Kosygin's four-day visit to Pyongyang in February 1965. Following these visits, the Russians signed two new defense agreements with North Korea, stepped up aid for more than fifty advanced industrial projects in North Korea, and greatly expanded trade and arms supplies. By the early 1970s, Moscow had become Pyongyang's largest trading partner and its most important arms supplier.[22] Two factors were crucial for this substantial improvement in Soviet–North Korean relations. First, the North Koreans must have come to the conclusion that they needed improved relations with the Russians for economic and military reasons. Khrushchev's decision to cut drastically economic and technical assistance in 1963 was disastrous for North Korea's national defense capability. At the same time, the United States was helping to modernize the South Korean armed forces, and Japan was reasserting its traditional economic interests in South Korea.[23] The North Korean leaders realized that Peking was not a satisfactory alternative to Moscow for technical and military assistance.

Second, North Korean relations with Peking began to deteriorate during the Cultural Revolution in China. In

1966 the North Korean press published an explicit criticism of Chinese ideographs, saying that they symbolized linguistic backwardness and that the Korean people should be proud of their phonetic alphabet and should not waste time trying to learn the Chinese symbols. During the Cultural Revolution, Chinese Red Guard posters accused Kim Il Sung himself of being "a millionaire, an aristocrat and a leading bourgeois element."[24] In 1969, there were reports of frontier incidents and of Chinese claims against North Korean territory on the remote stretches of their Manchurian border.

More recently, however, particularly during 1975 and 1976, there have been many signs of a new strain in Soviet–North Korean relations. The most dramatic evidence of this was Kim's failure to visit Moscow in the spring and summer of 1975, after a tour that took him to China, Eastern Europe, and North Africa. It was his first trip outside Korea in ten years. The only close Soviet ally Kim visited was Bulgaria, and the June 5, 1975, North Korean–Bulgarian communiqué suggested that there were substantial differences between the two sides.[25] Throughout his tour, Kim went out of his way to emphasize his independence from other communist powers and his identification with the Third World.

Whether the Russians snubbed Kim or Kim snubbed Moscow is unclear. A high-ranking Soviet official told me in the summer of 1975 that Moscow asked Kim to defer his planned visit to Russia until later in the year because Soviet officials were too busy to see him at that time. Several other Soviet officials described Kim to me as a "hot potato," whom they had best let the Chinese handle first.

Since the summer of 1975, there have been further indications of strain in the Moscow-Pyongyang relationship. Both Soviet and North Korean media have consistently played down anniversary occasions that in the past have been utilized to stress the friendly relations between the two states. For example, on the thirtieth anniversary of Korea's liberation from Japan in August 1975, North Korean comment played down Soviet assistance to Korea in and since 1945.

Also, in contrast to past quinquennial liberation anniversaries, no high-level Soviet delegation traveled to North Korea for the occasion.[26] The Russians did not send a delegation to Pyongyang either for the twenty-seventh anniversary of the nation's founding on September 8, 1975, or for the thirtieth anniversary of the Korean Workers' Party in October 1975. On that latter occasion, no top Soviet leaders attended the North Korean ambassador's reception in Moscow to commemorate the occasion. Moreover, only three communist states sent delegations to Pyongyang for the anniversary— Rumania, Cuba, and Hungary—and Kim Il Sung snubbed the Hungarian delegation.[27] The chill in Soviet–North Korean relations was also obvious in Pyongyang's very cool treatment of the fifty-eighth anniversary of the Russian Revolution in November 1975.[28]

What effect these new strains have had on Soviet–North Korean economic and military relations is still not clear. There is some indication that Moscow's formerly dominant role as Pyongyang's major arms supplier is now being challenged by Peking. South Korean officials told me during a visit to Seoul in the summer of 1976 that the quantity of Soviet military assistance to North Korea has been declining while Chinese military assistance is increasing. In or around 1972, 80 percent of North Korean military assistance came from the Soviet Union and the rest from China. Since early 1975, however, 50 percent of North Korea's military equipment has come from Russia and 50 percent from China.

Economic relations between the two countries also seem troubled. Pyongyang is estimated to have defaulted on 700 million dollars worth of credits from the Russians, and there is as yet no indication whether or how this debt will be repaid.[29] This 700 million represents almost half of the total 2.1 billion dollar foreign debt that North Korea has accumulated.

Yet another indication of the new chill in Soviet–North Korean relations is the effort by Kim Il Sung since 1973 to join the so-called nonaligned bloc and to cultivate relations with the Afro-Asian countries. In 1976 alone, as of June,

North Korea had sent forty-eight delegations to fifty-one of the nonaligned countries and had received visits from forty-two of those countries. Pyongyang, despite its own economic difficulties, had sent $8 million in aid to Third World states. Moreover, North Korea has used its new standing among the nonaligned to issue thinly veiled warnings against manipulation by the "big powers."[30]

There seem to be several reasons for the new chill in Soviet–North Korean relations. First, North Korea has moved closer to Peking. In April 1975, Kim Il Sung visited China for eight days and was received personally by Mao Tse-tung. Banquet speeches and a joint communiqué referred to a complete identity of views.[31] In September 1975, Politburo member Chang Chun-chiao paid a six-day visit to North Korea, and at the end of the visit it was again announced that there was "a complete consensus of views" on questions of common concern.[32] In October 1975, Peking, unlike Moscow, honored the Korean Workers' Party anniversary with an editorial in the main party newspaper, *People's Daily,* and a Chinese leadership turnout at the North Korean reception in Peking was led by five Politburo members, including Chang Chun-chiao.[33]

A second reason for the strain in Soviet–North Korean relations appears to be Moscow's reluctance to give whole-hearted support to Pyongyang's strategy for reunification. Soviet media and leaders do not treat the Korean issue as one of high priority on their diplomatic agenda. For example, in Brezhnev's lengthy report on the world situation to the twenty-fifth CPSU Congress in February 1976, the Soviet leader made no reference at all to the Korean question, and he included only one reference to Pyongyang in a ceremonial list of "fraternal socialist states."[34]

Even more revealing, however, is the sharp difference in tone and content between the occasional Soviet commentaries on Korea and those of North Korea itself. At a time when Pyongyang, supported by Peking, was claiming that North Korea was the "sole sovereign state" on the Korean peninsula, Moscow was still talking about an end to military confrontation being in accord with the interests of the peoples of "both Korean states," thus implicitly rejecting Pyongyang's claim that South Korea was not a sovereign state.[35] While Pyongyang was contending that its dialogue with South Korea was on the point of rupture, Moscow was offering an upbeat assessment of the dialogue.[36] While Pyongyang customarily refers to the need for "independent" reunification of Korea, a reunification to be achieved by the Koreans themselves, Moscow almost always drops the phrase "independent," thus signaling its intention to be part of any future negotiations on the Korean question.[37]

There also appear to be differences of view between Moscow and Pyongyang on former Secretary Kissinger's call for an international conference to discuss the Korean problem. Pyongyang responded negatively to Kissinger's proposals for a four-power conference among the signatories of the Korean armistice to discuss ways of preserving the armistice agreement; it called instead for direct negotiations between North Korea and the United States, thus bypassing South Korea. But Moscow has not similarly denounced Kissinger's proposals.[38] While Pyongyang no longer refers to the need for a North-South peace agreement, emphasizing instead direct negotiations with the United States, the Soviets continue to call such a North-South agreement indispensable for a successful solution of the Korean problem.[39]

In sum, Moscow has refused to endorse Pyongyang's recent efforts to question South Korea's legitimacy; it has refused to echo somber North Korean assessments of the North-South dialogue; and it has refused to go along with Pyongyang's cavalier responses to American proposals for firming up the armistice. In private, Soviet specialists say that a "two Koreas" solution is the only solution to the Korean problem. On a number of recent occasions, despite obvious disapproval from Pyongyang, the Russians have admitted South Korean sportsmen and other groups to Moscow in order to participate in international conferences.[40] Indeed, one of the principal sources of strain between Moscow and Pyongyang seems to be North Korea's fear that

Moscow may yet recognize the South Korean government, a fear strengthened by the American proposal for cross-recognition of the two Koreas by the great powers. In January 1975, shortly after the cross-recognition proposal was advanced by Assistant Secretary of State for East Asian Affairs, Philip Habib, a North Korean party newspaper warned that socialist states "cannot deal with puppets . . . still less recognize them."[41] It was later that year that Pyongyang enunciated its position that it was the "sole sovereign state" on the Korean peninsula—a position yet to be embraced by the Russians.

These differences seem to reflect a more basic incompatibility of interests between Moscow and Pyongyang. The Soviet leaders do not trust the North Korean dictator, Kim Il Sung, and they probably do not desire a unified, communist Korea. Under present circumstances, so long as American troops are committed to the defense of South Korea, unification could only come about through a war in which both the Soviet Union and the United States would become involved automatically as a result of their respective treaty commitments.

The Russians could not afford to let Pyongyang win or lose such a war.

A North Korean loss in a new Korean war would have profound political and psychological consequences among the Soviet Union's other allies and treaty partners. A North Korean victory would run the risk of a Soviet-American military confrontation, end the détente, carry the risk of Chinese intervention, and lead to great pressure within Japan for Japanese remilitarization—all of which would be severely detrimental to Soviet interests. But even if North Korea could somehow come to dominate South Korea by means of a short war, a unified communist Korea might eventually gravitate toward Peking and severely complicate Soviet security problems on its southern flank. At the very least, if Korea were to be unified by the North, Soviet leverage on North Korea would be greatly reduced because the North would no longer have to fear American troops and a hostile

South Korean army on its border. Thus, there are no compelling reasons for Moscow to support North Korean efforts to unify all of Korea, much less to risk a war in the process.

While Soviet–North Korean relations thus remain rather cool, it seems unlikely that there will be an open break. Each side needs the other. Moscow, for its part, fears driving Pyongyang too far into the waiting embrace of Peking. For this reason also the Russians avoid any public approval of a "two Koreas" solution and generally go through the motions of supporting North Korean positions, albeit in a very restrained manner. North Korea, on the other hand, has no alternative to Soviet economic and technical assistance, particularly now that it has defaulted on many of its international obligations. Indeed, it is possible that North Korean economic dependence on Moscow may grow now that Pyongyang's economic opening to Japan and Western Europe has been thrown into doubt as a result of Pyongyang's default.[42]

Moreover, North Korea is dependent on Soviet technology for modernizing an economy that in the past was overly dependent on military-oriented heavy industry. As of 1974, the Soviets were building more than thirty industrial enterprises in North Korea, and a Soviet-Korean Intergovernmental Commission for Economic and Scientific-Technical Questions, established in 1967, was meeting twice a year. In addition, 580 Soviet specialists were at construction sites in North Korea, and the volume of trade turnover had increased substantially from the late 1950s. The Russians claimed that their assistance to North Korea would make it possible to increase the production of steel, electric power, and rolled products by 30 percent to 40 percent.[43]

Pyongyang also remains heavily dependent on Moscow for some of its oil requirements, most of its modern jet aircraft, and its air defense system. Only military equipment of intermediate technology, such as howitzers, tank parts, and some types of vessels, can be manufactured by the North Koreans themselves. Soviet military assistance to the North continues, albeit at an apparently reduced level. Since 1974,

Moscow has sent Pyongyang eighty-one aircraft including MIG-21s, AN-2s, and AN-24s, along with $593 million worth of economic credits for some twenty industrial projects.

At the same time, it is apparent that Moscow keeps a tight rein on its North Korean clients. Moscow has been unwilling to provide North Korea with its most advanced aircraft, either MIG-23s or 25s, for example; it has also refused to supply Pyongyang with an electronic or a mobile air defense system, with amphibious landing craft, with armored personnel carriers suited for rapid mobile war, or with ground-to-ground missiles of considerable range. At the same time, however, Moscow has provided many of these weapons or weapons systems to Syria and Egypt.[44] It is thus apparent that it is not eager to equip Pyongyang with weapons systems that could turn the balance of power in its favor and tempt North Korea to launch a new war on the Korean peninsula. To sum up, the Soviet–North Korean relationship resembles more a marriage of convenience than a close alliance, and it is beset with chronic strain and tension.

Soviet policy in Korea during the foreseeable future will probably avoid each of two extremes. On the one hand, Moscow will not support or encourage North Korean military action against South Korea, and it will be deeply concerned about any North Korean actions that could embroil the Soviet Union in a war in Korea. Moscow seems to have been disturbed by the slaying of two American soldiers at the DMZ in August 1976, an incident that prompted an American show of strength. At the other extreme, Moscow will not recognize South Korea, publicly advocate a policy of "two Koreas," or pressure North Korea to recognize South Korea. The Russians will avoid the first course of action so as not to damage their relations with the United States and Japan and because the potential gains are not worth the potential costs. They will avoid the second course of action so as not to drive North Korea into the arms of China and because the potential gains from courting South Korea are not so great as to risk alienating North Korea.

The Soviet Union and Southern Asia

Although Moscow did have high hopes of establishing a bridgehead in Indochina through its support of the Hanoi government's conquest of South Vietnam, recent trends in that area cannot be entirely to Moscow's satisfaction. Hanoi, while intent on maintaining good relations with Moscow, has refused to echo Moscow's call for an anti-Chinese collective security pact, has gone out of its way to improve its relations with its ASEAN neighbors, and, most important of all, has demonstrated great interest in a rapprochement with the United States. Hanoi is evidently attaching first priority to rebuilding its war-ravaged economy, and it wants to attract American and Western capital to aid in this effort. Hanoi has also sought to defuse the territorial conflicts it has with China over the Spratly and Paracel Islands. Thus, the Vietnamese communists are seeking to maneuver between Peking, Washington, and Moscow rather than to tilt one-sidedly toward the Russians. The Laotian communists are likely to follow the same path. In Cambodia, the new communist government seems much closer to Peking than to any other foreign power.

Elsewhere in Southeast Asia, despite Moscow's recent efforts to improve its diplomatic and economic position in order to contain China, the Soviets have not achieved major successes anywhere. The ASEAN countries are, to be sure, interested in cultivating Moscow in order to take out a low-cost insurance policy against Chinese hostility. But nowhere in the region does Moscow have substantial influence. Moreover, in Australia and New Zealand, the new conservative governments, alarmed at the rapid expansion of the Soviet Pacific Fleet, have both moved closer to Peking.

Until the stunning and unexpected defeat of Indira Gandhi in the Indian elections in March 1977, the biggest Soviet success story in the Far East had been in New Delhi. But the new Indian Prime Minister, Morarji Desai, has already indicated that although he does not intend to abolish the Soviet-Indian Friendship Treaty of 1971, he is determined to improve relations with the United States. Indian relations with China were already showing some improvement even before the defeat of Indira Gandhi, and this trend may now accelerate. Thus, Soviet fortunes in India have been dealt a sharp setback.

Elsewhere on the Indian subcontinent, Soviet relations with Pakistan have been strained ever since Moscow openly supported India against Pakistan in the Bangladesh war of 1971. And the new Bangladesh government that came to power in 1976 has moved away from its earlier pro-Indian and pro-Soviet orientation to improve relations with Pakistan and China.

Conclusion

Are there any general explanations that can account for the generally low level of Soviet political influence in Asia? No doubt the Russians are hampered in the Far East by the fact that they are Europeans and generally regarded as outsiders. Unlike the Chinese, they have no cultural ties to any part of the region. Furthermore, the Russians have very little that anyone in the region wants. Their ideology is no longer exportable, and, unlike the Americans and the Japanese, they have little economic relevance to most of the countries in the region. Then too, in contrast to the situation in southern Africa, where the Russians can exploit the continuing racial struggle, or the Middle East, where the Russians can exploit the continuing conflict between Israel and the Arabs, the Far East does not provide any easily exploitable opportunities now that the Vietnam war is over and the region is relatively quiescent.

But a final factor in the poor Soviet showing in the Far East is the shortcomings of Moscow's own policy. By far the two biggest Soviet failures in the Far East have been in alienating China and in failing to exploit the opportunity to loosen Japan from its American alliance. These two failures have had a common denominator—a narrowly rigid concern with security. In the case of China, this has led to a massive military buildup on the Chinese border that virtually guarantees the impossibility of reaching an accommodation with Peking, even now that Mao is gone from the scene. In the case of Japan, this same mentality has led to a rigid position on the four southern islands that has deprived the Russians of any flexibility in their relationship with Tokyo.

To what can we attribute this rigid and self-defeating concern with security? Partly, no doubt, to a troubled Russian history, in which enemies have frequently invaded Russia through weakly defended frontiers. Partly to the influence of the Soviet military, which is probably advocating a hard-line approach on such matters. And partly, no doubt, to a characteristic Soviet overreaction to a genuine threat.

The great danger ahead is that in seeking to compensate for its relatively weak political position in the Far East, Moscow may try to develop a position of great military strength as a substitute. The large concentration of forces on the Chinese border, the rapid expansion of the Soviet Pacific Fleet, and the urgent plans to develop Siberia—all point in this direction. It is an ominous trend that bears watching.

Notes

1. See W. A. Douglas Jackson, *The Russo-Chinese Borderlands* (Princeton, N.J.: Van Nostrand, 1968), pp. 100-103.

2. For details on the buildup, see Thomas W. Robinson, "The Sino-Soviet Border Dispute," *The American Political Science Review* 66, no. 4 (December 1972): 1175-1202.

3. See the testimony to the Committee on International Relations of the House of Representatives by Morton I. Abramowitz, Deputy Assistant Secretary of Defense, East Asia and Pacific Affairs, April 6, 1976, reprinted in *Contemporary China*, December 1976.

4. *New York Times*, April 5, 1977, p. 3.

5. In 1946, Chou En-lai told General Marshall that a communist China would of course tilt towards Moscow but "how far depends on you."

6. *Peking Review*, October 22, 1976, p. 18.

7. Ibid., November 5, 1976, p. 18.

8. Ibid., December 3, 1976, p. 21.

9. Ibid., January 14, 1977, p. 31.

10. Ibid., February 11, 1977, and February 25, 1977.

11. Ibid., March 4, 1977.

12. *Pravda*, February 10, 1977, article by "Commentator," and *Pravda* article by Georgiev on March 19, 1977.

13. *Peking Review*, January 28, 1977, p. 13.

14. *Far Eastern Economic Review*, February 4, 1977, p. 9.

15. "Averting Moscow-Peking Rapprochement," *Pacific Community* 8, no. 1 (October 1976).

16. Robert Dernberger, "China's Economic Evolution and its Implications for the International System in the 1980's," Council on Foreign Relations, 1980's Project.

17. The paragraph above is based on John J. Stephan, "The Kurile Islands: Japan Versus Russia," *Pacific Community* 7, no. 3 (April 1976): 311-330.

18. Ibid.

19. For a balanced and sober appraisal of the Soviet military buildup, see John Erickson, "Soviet Military Capabilities," *Current History* 71, no. 420 (October 1976): 97-100.

20. For the details, see Joungwon Alexander Kim, "Soviet Policy in North Korea," *World Politics* 22, no. 2 (January 1970): 237-254.

21. See B. C. Koh, "North Korea and the Sino-Soviet Schism," *Western Political Quarterly* 22, no. 4 (December 1969): 940-962.

22. See David Rees, "The New Pressures from North Korea,"*Conflict Studies*, no. 3 (February-March, 1970); *New York Times*, April 20, 1969; also Jane P. Shapiro, "Soviet Policy Towards North Korea and Korean Unification," *Pacific Affairs* 48, no. 3 (Fall 1975): 335-352.

23. See Shapiro, "Soviet Policy Towards North Korea."

24. Rees, "New Pressures from North Korea."

25. U. S. Executive Office of the President, Foreign Broadcast Information Service, *Trends*, June 11, 1975.

26. FBIS *Trends*, August 20, 1975, p. 21.

27. FBIS *Trends*, October 16, 1975, p. 16; also ibid., September 10, 1975, p. 20.

28. FBIS *Trends,* November 12, 1975, p. 11.

29. A North Korean minister visited Moscow in January 1977, presumably to discuss future economic relations, but no details have been announced.

30. FBIS *Trends,* October 16, 1975, p. 15.

31. FBIS *Trends,* April 30, 1975, p. 9.

32. FBIS *Trends,* October 1, 1975, pp. 4-5.

33. FBIS *Trends,* October 22, 1975, p. 16.

34. See Leonid Brezhnev, Press release on the "World Situation," USSR Mission to the UN, February 25, 1976.

35. FBIS *Trends,* November 5, 1975, p. 23.

36. Ibid.

37. The Chinese first called attention to this. See FBIS *Trends,* October 30, 1975. My own spot check of Soviet media on Korea generally corroborated the Chinese charge.

38. FBIS *Trends,* October 1, 1975, p. 2.

39. FBIS *Trends,* August 20, 1975, p. 23.

40. See Donald Zagoria and Young Kun Kim, "North Korea and the Major Powers," in *The Two Koreas in East Asian Affairs,* ed. William J. Barnds (New York: NYU Press, 1976).

41. FBIS *Trends,* January 15, 1975, p. 30.

42. I was told during a visit to Japan in June 1976 that no Japanese exporters were applying for export insurance for sales to North Korea, an indication that North Korean credit is now suspect.

43. See "A Quarter of a Century of Friendship and Cooperation: On the 25th Anniversary of the Agreement on Economic and Cultural Cooperation Between the USSR and the DPRK," *Problems of the Far East* (Moscow), no. 1, 1974, translated in Joint Publications Research Service, no. 61955, May 9, 1974.

44. I am indebted to Arnold Horelick of the Rand Corporation for this information as well as for a number of valuable insights into Soviet policy in the Far East.

5. Japan and Asia: Growing Entanglement

Donald C. Hellmann

Three decades after catastrophic defeat and astonishing economic growth, Japan is a global as well as a regional power and plays a central, but passive, role in Asian international relations. The dramatic and unexpected events that have fundamentally altered and complicated the international landscape since 1970 have had a peculiarly potent, but not widely appreciated, impact on Tokyo. In recent years, the most visible changes in Japanese foreign policy in Asia have involved relations with the "great powers": the United States, the Soviet Union, and China. Accordingly, much concern about Japan's role in the world has focused on the nature of a new power balance in a "multipolar world." Similarly, the breakdown in the Bretton Woods monetary system and the destabilizing effects of the oil crisis have led to the consideration of Tokyo's foreign policy from a global perspective and away from a direct concern for Japan's role in Asia. At the same time, Japan has also tended to give priority to relations with the great powers and to the energy crisis, especially in public pronouncements on the direction of the nation's foreign policy. This orientation has obscured some highly significant developments that have pulled Japan more deeply into East Asian affairs than at any time since World War II and that will profoundly shape the future of Japan's international actions.

To understand the regional dimension of Japanese foreign policy and the ways it is linked to global affairs, it is essential to note three of the most distinctive features of the current international situation. First, and most importantly, many significant changes (e.g., the collapse of Indochina, the oil crisis, the spread of nuclear weapons, the breakdown of the Bretton Woods monetary system) took place not out of conscious choice by the superpowers, but as a result of developments beyond their control. Not only have both superpowers shown incapacities to control events on a global basis, but both are also groping for new instruments for influence—especially in Asia. These circumstances make it essential to look beyond the articulated aims and the existing alliances of all nations—especially Japan—to identify the underlying patterns of economic and diplomatic interaction that establish the parameters for diplomatic choice. Second, in contrast to the situation in Europe, the political-strategic situation in Asia today is much more fluid and indeterminate. There is an inherent instability in the region rooted, inter alia, in the unpredictability of China, a history of international conflict spanning almost a century, and the presence of smaller nations such as the two Koreas, Vietnam, and Taiwan, which now have both the political commitment and the national potential for independent military-political actions. Third, the growing tendency of poorer countries to use their political control over primary resources to bring about "a new economic order" or for explicitly political ends, to date most dramatically illustrated by the oil embargo, places added strain on the fragile international economic order. Further, it forces countries such as Japan, which are truly dependent on access to critical raw materials, to link closely politics and economics in devising their policies toward Third World nations. The emergence of scarcity in an era of nuclear proliferation and polymorphous violence challenges the basic assumptions of Japan's "economic diplomacy," especially in regard to Asia.

Japan's role in intra-Asian relations will be considered in

this broad context from three perspectives. First, the economic ties between Japan and the other countries in the region are examined to evaluate the impact of the sweeping changes during the decade of the 1970s and to demonstrate the strength of the web linking Japan to East Asia. After a brief summary and analysis of the political-diplomatic actions of Japan in the region during this same period in order to delineate another aspect of Japanese entanglement, the way in which Asian issues have become ensnared in Japanese domestic politics is evaluated and the prospects for a more active and expanded political-strategic role for Tokyo in the region are explained.

Japan: An Asian or a Global Power?

Is Japan really an Asian nation? This question, at first glance trivial because of the elementary facts of geography and history, must be treated seriously and answered with care. In the first place, Japan, which was a "great power" throughout the first half of the twentieth century, pursued international status after 1945 almost exclusively in terms of the alliance with the United States and acceptance within the group of industrialized Western nations. Not only have the Japanese themselves given priority to a non-Asian policy, but there has been an almost universal tendency among American statesmen and commentators to classify Japan with the industrial and democratic countries of the West. Two examples are particularly noteworthy. Several years ago, Secretary of State Kissinger announced his hopes for "a New Atlantic Charter, plus Japan," in one stroke providing a mind-boggling distortion of the world geopolitical map and confusing the Japanese. In the early 1970s, a number of prominent American businessmen, politicians, and scholars set up an organization called the Trilateral Commission to promote communication among Japanese, United States, and Western European elites in order to facilitate and to manage solutions of the world's economic and political problems. While there was (and in some circles still is) a certain plausibility and attraction to the idea that advanced

industrial societies will provide political as well as economic
leadership in an affluent new world, this has been seriously
challenged by the events of the last few years. The effectiveness of OPEC demonstrated the political-economic clout of
one sector of the Third World; and the persistence of appall-
ing poverty in what seems to be a chronically impoverished
"Fourth World," the retreat of the United States from global
leadership, and the persistence of political (and ideological)
conflicts in international affairs have all shattered the vision
of a benignly evolving new world order. Even more importantly in terms of this chapter, the emphasis explicit in this
approach to one aspect of Japan's international posture
(global economic interdependence) has given short shrift to
the strong Asian political dimension of Japanese diplomacy
and to some basic patterns of trade, aid, and investment that
skew Tokyo's policy in a regional direction.

Two patterns of trade development since 1970 are especially dramatic in underscoring the Asian orientation of Japan
and the mounting dependence of Tokyo on trade with the
more politically volatile and unpredictable developing nations. Table 1 compares Japan's trade with the European
Economic Community with its trade with South Korea,
Taiwan, and Hong Kong. It should be noted that the EEC
constitutes a market fifty to sixty times the size of this
noncommunist area of Asia and that during the early 1970s
Japan had notable success in expanding trade with Europe.
It should also be noted that for part of this period Japan had
very strained diplomatic relations with South Korea and no
diplomatic ties with Taiwan after September 1972. That
Tokyo now does almost ninety percent as much trade with
two small developing nations and a city-colony in Asia (all
resource-poor) as is done with the entire European Economic Community provides an elemental lesson in international
affairs that we all should review.[1]

Japan continues to dominate trade in the East Asian
region to a startling degree. During the 1950s and 1960s,
despite vestigial anti-Japanese feelings from World War II

Table 1

JAPAN'S TRADE WITH THE EUROPEAN ECONOMIC COMMUNITY
vs.
JAPAN'S TRADE WITH SOUTH KOREA, TAIWAN, AND HONG KONG
(In millions of U.S. dollars)

	EEC			Per cent of Japan's Total Trade	South Korea, Taiwan, Hong Kong			Per cent of Japan's Total Trade	Per cent of S.K.,T., H.K. Total Trade ÷ EEC Total Trade
	Exports	Imports	Total		Exports	Imports	Total		
1970	1,847.4	1,542.3	3,389.7	8.8	2,218.9	571.6	2,790.5	7.3	83
1971	2,278.4	1,593.1	3,871.5	8.8	2,571.0	656.4	3,227.4	7.4	84
1972	3,280.6	1,943.4	5,224.0	10.0	2,984.1	967.2	3,951.3	7.6	76
1973	4,378.2	3,152.4	7,530.6	10.0	4,558.5	2,384.9	6,943.4	9.2	92
1974	5,926.6	3,953.7	9,880.3	8.4	6,023.2	2,793.5	8,816.7	7.5	89
1975	5,615.6	3,336.2	8,951.8	7.9	5,443.2	2,363.0	7,806.2	6.9	87

Source: International Monetary Fund, Direction of Trade, 1970-74, July, 1976

and conditions of almost continuous war and political disruption, Japan moved into a commanding trade position, displacing the former European colonial powers, completely overshadowing China, and eventually surpassing the United States. As indicated in table 2, there has been remarkable continuity in this earlier pattern during the turbulent years of the early 1970s. Indeed, Japan has substantially expanded its position of leadership to the point that it now does almost as much trade with the region as the next seven extraregional trading partners combined.[2]

Just how fully the Japanese dominate intraregional trade is even more evident in the bilateral trade patterns between East Asian countries and Japan. For almost a decade, Japan has been the first or second leading trading partner of every country in the region, and, as seen in table 3, this situation continued in 1974 in the face of the widespread disruptions of the world economy and rather spectacular rates of economic growth in all noncommunist countries in the region except for Burma. The trade dependence of the nations of the region on Japan has reached proportions that transcend simply commercial relations, as Prime Minister Tanaka discovered to his surprise on his trip to Southeast Asia in early 1974. Whatever the extent of Japan's global economic

Table 2

PERCENTAGE SHARES OF MAJOR TRADING COUNTRIES IN THE TOTAL
TRADE OF THE EAST ASIAN REGION,a 1958-74
(In millions of U.S. dollars)

	Japan	United Kingdom	West Germany	France	Netherlands	Australia	China	United States
1958 Total Trade	1,046.1	690.4	553.7	270.0	236.9	233.7	231.2	1,495.9
Per cent	9.0	6.0	4.8	2.3	2.0	2.0	1.0	12.9
1960 Total Trade	1,486.4	765.9	645.0	316.3	218.1	234.2	233.0	1,634.2
Per cent	11.3	6.0	4.9	2.4	1.7	1.8	1.0	12.4
1965 Total Trade	2,971.1	784.4	721.9	400.3	440.0	503.7	177.6	2,252.9
Per cent	20.0	5.4	5.0	2.8	3.0	3.5	1.2	15.6
1969 Total Trade	5,857.8	935.9	1,114.9	543.6	350.5	673.8	351.0	4,091.89
Per cent	27.4	4.4	5.2	2.5	1.6	3.2	1.6	19.1
1970 Total Trade	6,850.2	1,012.7	1,204.7	546.3	377.4	715.5	272.3	4,664.3
Per cent	28.4	4.2	5.0	2.2	1.6	3.0	1.1	19.2
1971 Total Trade	7,773.3	1,092.5	1,309.2	593.6	454.9	565.9	254.5	5,202.8
Per cent	28.7	4.0	4.8	2.2	1.7	2.4	.9	19.2
1972 Total Trade	9,513.9	1,188.3	1,459.2	635.1	483.0	849.4	299.1	6,728.3
Per cent	28.6	3.7	4.5	2.0	1.5	2.6	.9	20.8
1973 Total Trade	16,333.2	1,884.6	2,700.7	1,166.7	815.7	1,392.2	596.3	10,726.2
Per cent	30.6	3.5	5.1	2.2	1.5	2.6	1.1	20.1
1974 Total Trade	25,331.7	2,416.3	3,569.0	1,600.3	1,192.0	2,285.7	834.7	15,736.0
Per cent	30.3	2.9	4.3	2.0	1.4	2.7	1.0	18.8

aIncludes Burma, Cambodia, Communist China, Nationalist China, Indonesia, North Korea, South
Korea, Laos, Malaysia (Malaya, Malaysia-Singapore), the Philippines, Singapore, Thailand,
North Vietnam, and South Vietnam, Brunei.

Sources: International Monetary Fund and International Bank for Reconstruction and
Development, Direction of Trade, 1958-62, 1963-67, 1969-73, 1970-74.

Table 3

TRADE OF EAST ASIAN COUNTRIES WITH JAPAN AS A PERCENTAGE
OF THEIR TOTAL TRADE, 1974
(In millions of U.S. dollars)

Country[a]	Exports		Imports		Total		Rank (total trade)
	Amount	%	Amount	%	Amount	%	
Brunei	802.23	89.70	38.30	23.30	840.53	79.40	1
China	1,185.60	22.79	2,181.60	32.79	3,367.20	28.40	1
Taiwan	849.09	15.38	2,221.23	31.81	3,070.32	24.56	2
Indonesia	3,954.80	53.26	1,139.20	30.35	5,094.00	45.56	1
Korea	1,380.19	30.94	2,620.55	36.83	4,000.74	35.39	1
Malaysia	713.92	16.90	915.46	22.00	1,629.38	19.43	1
North Korea	98.84	40.70	276.99	33.10	375.83	34.85	1
Philippines[b]	932.40	34.90	923.90	26.90	1,856.30	30.40	2
Singapore	637.60	11.00	1,528.50	18.20	2,166.10	15.27	1
Thailand	639.20	25.90	1,009.75	32.70	1,648.95	29.66	1

[a]Burma, Cambodia, Laos have been omitted because they are not statistically significant. North and South Vietnam are omitted because they are sui generis.
Source: International Monetary Fund, Direction of Trade, 1970-74.
[b]Virtually equal to the U.S.

role and the aversion of Tokyo's leaders to power politics, the size and scope of the nation's stake in the region—measured simply in terms of trade figures—make Japanese political involvement in the problems of East Asia all but inevitable. Because this network of trade ties has been generated largely by forces of the marketplace, it has been erroneously downgraded as a critical dimension in Japanese foreign policy.

The size of Japanese trade looks substantial from all of the capitals of Asia, and Asian trade is also important from the viewpoint of Tokyo. As shown in table 4, despite the enormous expansion of Japanese trade on a global basis since 1958 (twentyfold in nominal terms), the amount taken by the Asian region in 1975 had risen to 20.9 percent of Japan's total trade, virtually identical with the level of Japanese-American trade. The rise in the amount of Japan's trade taken by the Asian region has taken place entirely during the decade of the 1970s. There are two basic reasons: the sharp growth of trade with China following the normalization of diplomatic relations with Peking (see table 5) and the steep rise in the price of oil and other primary products,

Table 4

JAPAN'S TRADE WITH EAST ASIAN REGION,[a] 1958-74

Year	Japan's Trade with Region (in millions of U.S. dollars)	Per Cent of Japan's Total Trade
1958	1,046.1	17.7
1960	1,486.4	17.4
1965	2,970.4	19.1
1969	5,857.8	18.9
1970	6,850.2	17.9
1971	7,777.3	17.7
1972	9,513.9	18.3
1973	16,333.2	21.7
1974	25,331.7	21.5
1975	23,771.4	20.9

[a]Includes: China, Indonesia, Philippines, S. Korea, Thailand, Taiwan, Malaysia, S. Vietnam, Burma, N. Vietnam, Cambodia, N. Korea, Singapore, Laos, and Brunei.
    Sources: Ministry of Finance, Japanese Government, Boeiki Nenkan (Trade Annual), 1974, 1975; International Monetary Fund, Direction of Trade, 1958-62, 1963-67, 1968-72, 1969-73, 1970-74, July 1976.

Table 5

SINO-JAPANESE TRADE, 1969-74

Year	Japan's trade with China (in millions of U.S. dollars)			Per cent of total Japanese trade	Per cent of total Chinese trade
	Exports	Imports	Total		
1960	2.7	20.7	23.4	.3	.6
1965	245.3	224.7	470.0	2.8	17.6
1969	390.8	234.5	625.3	2.0	19.5
1970	568.9	253.8	822.7	2.2	23.0
1971	578.5	323.3	901.8	2.1	23.6
1972	609.7	491.1	1,100.8	2.1	23.1
1973	1,042.3	974.2	2,016.5	2.7	24.1
1974	1,983.2	1,304.0	3,287.2	2.8	27.7
1975	2,258.2	1,529.4	3,787.6	3.3	N.A.

Sources: International Monetary Fund, Direction of Trade, 1958-62, 1963-67, 1969-73, 1970-74, July 1976.

which has drastically altered the trade pattern between Japan and the developing countries. Since the late 1960s Japan's trade with industrialized countries has dropped from slightly more than 50 percent of its total trade to approximately 35 percent. During this same period, trade with the less-developed world has risen from 35 to 48 percent. In short, trade has increasingly tied Japan to the politically volatile Third World in general and the countries of Asia in particular.[3]

Japan is also linked to Asia through aid and economically oriented multilateral organizations such as the Asian Development Bank—which have increasingly been dominated by the Japanese. The sizable Japanese aid program has been effectively an aid program to Asia. In terms of Japan's official development assistance (grants, soft loans, and technical assistance), 98 percent was concentrated in Asia in 1972. The Asian component had dropped to 87 percent by 1974, but this astonishing concentration within the region offers further evidence that Japan is indeed an Asian power. Moreover, much of this recent aid has been directed toward two countries, Indonesia and South Korea, and has been extended in ways that are integrated with the governmental development programs in both nations. The magnitude and form of this assistance make it increasingly difficult for the Japanese to remain free from political entanglements with these countries. In addition, during the early 1970s, the Japanese made substantial direct investments throughout the region, and again, in Indonesia and South Korea, they have become the dominant international economic force. From any viewpoint, it is evident that Japan will remain the preeminent economic force in East Asia for the foreseeable future.

Under these circumstances it is difficult to see how Tokyo can indefinitely remain aloof from international politics in the region and from the concomitant security responsibilities, especially in view of the high probability for political conflict in the region and the increasingly uncertain roles of the superpowers in such conflicts. While there is no short-term economic *necessity* for Japan to become involved in power politics in the region, in a world of scarcity in which developing states have adopted a militantly nationalist posture with regard to resources and investments, the long-term pressures will be substantial. The web of economic intercourse has drawn Japan more deeply into regional affairs, and another web of political and diplomatic ties now reinforces this orientation.

Japan: Political Regionalism in an Interdependent World

Until 1971, Japan's political relations in East Asia were almost entirely subsumed under the American alliance. To be sure, the Foreign Ministry "blue books" regularly asserted that Japan as an Asian nation had a special place in Asia, and by far the largest number of diplomatic initiatives undertaken were in regard to the region. But Japan, as I have argued elsewhere, functioned more as a trading company than a nation, and any truly major political initiatives (e.g., recognition of Peking) were scrupulously avoided. Events commencing in 1971 have forced Japan into somewhat bolder policies. The so-called Nixon shocks in the summer of that year left the Japanese with virtually no choice but to recognize Peking; the anti-Japanese sentiment manifested in Prime Minister Tanaka's "goodwill visit" to Southeast Asia in early 1974 forced reconsideration of "economic diplomacy"; the collapse of South Vietnam led to closer coordination with the United States regarding the defense of South Korea; and the Peking-Moscow-Tokyo triangular diplomacy led Japan to stumble on a number of political issues (e.g., the northern territories question, the development of Siberian resources, and a protracted haggle with Peking over a treaty of peace and friendship). As American military power in the region is reduced and as our future intentions remain more indeterminate than in the recent past, the Japanese have taken modest steps to play a more independent political role in Asia. Progress has been incremental, there clearly is no consensus about long-term goals, and the Foreign Ministry's so-called policy of equidistance is, on close inspection, little more than a euphemism for keeping all options open and avoiding involvement. Nevertheless, steps have been taken that do establish a new threshold of involvement, and these have been taken primarily in Northeast Asia.

Sino-Japanese relations continue to be shaped by the dynamics of international and domestic events rather than any carefully calculated strategem in Peking or Tokyo.

Recognition of China by Japan came only after Peking was admitted to the United Nations, after every major world power had recognized or "made peace" with the Chinese, and when continued refusal by Japan to act would have created an adversary relationship of uncertain and potentially high cost. After recognition, trade burgeoned (table 5), and Japan retained its position as the leading trading partner of Peking, a position it has held since 1964. The size and scope of China's trade with Japan (especially the import of technology) has created of dependence on Tokyo, but the possibility for substantial future oil exports and the potential for the political manipulation of trade serve as countervailing influences. Whether the expansion of trade and other lines of communication will in the long run have a salutary influence on bilateral relations is clearly problematical, but they have given a salience to this relationship that inevitably will touch other aspects of Japan's diplomacy in Asia. Peking readily accepts this fact, but in the continuing debate in Tokyo over acceptance of a regional "anti-hegemony clause" in the proposed peace treaty, the Japanese have shown extreme reluctance even to acknowledge that they are actively part of the power balance in East Asia. Whether the peace treaty is finalized has now become largely a function of the international political situations in both Tokyo and Peking.

The issue of Taiwan, seemingly disposed of in 1972, lingers on, with an unofficial Japanese diplomatic delegation in Taipei, a level of bilateral trade equal to that with the mainland, and the restoration of regular airline connections. Thus, Japan's "two Chinas" policy of the 1960s persists, albeit stood on its head. The result of all these changes has less to do with reducing the potential for conflict than with greatly intensifying and expanding the range of contacts. Perhaps the most significant legacy of expanded relations with China has been to pull Japan more deeply into regional affairs on all levels.

Japan's relations with South Korea during recent years have been one of the most eventful and interesting chapters

in postwar Japanese diplomacy. Bilateral ties have been
marred by two extraordinary incidents: a bizarre kidnapping
of a leading South Korean opposition politician from a
Tokyo hotel (purportedly by the Korean CIA) and the
assassination of the wife of ROK President Park Chung Hee
by a Korean resident of Japan. Both incidents had major
political repercussions in each country (including the sack-
ing of the Japanese embassy in Seoul) in ways that greatly
intensified and complicated all levels of contact. At the same
time, there have been regular high-level governmental and
private conferences, massive tourist exchanges, and an enormous expansion of bilateral trade. Japan has become the
major foreign investor in South Korea, and in addition to
massive private loans, there have been and will continue to
be annual government loans of at least $300 million by
Japan. Finally, the collapse of Saigon in 1975 led the
Japanese government to reconfirm a statement made in 1969
that "Korea's security is essential to Japan's " and to back off,
at least temporarily, from efforts to normalized relations
with North Korea. Again the scope and intensity of contacts
with South Korea have crossed a new threshold, which
cannot but lead Japan to face the realities of power politics
and the political tensions of Asia, which have been so
fortuitously avoided until now.

Japanese Domestic Politics and Asian Policy

At a moment when changes in the international scene
require flexible, new approaches by Tokyo, Japan's domestic political situation has entered a period of fluidity and
uncertainty that cannot but profoundly influence its policy
toward Asia. Shaken by a series of scandals culminating in
the Lockheed bribery affair, the Liberal-Democratic Party,
which has ruled Japan since the occupation, is beset by bitter
intraparty differences and a decline in popular support that
make strong foreign policy leadership extremely improbable. Even if conservatives cling to power without having
to form a coalition with another party, severe internal
divisions will virtually prescribe bold policy actions. Fur-

thermore, the sharp differences among the four opposition parties insure that any left-leaning coalition government they may form would be even more inhibited from positive action than one led by the conservatives. In short, during at least the latter part of the 1970s, Japan's stalemated domestic political configuration will insure its continued passivity in international politics. Moreover, this internal political stalemate is aggravated by the fact that there is no strong consensus on the appropriate policy goals, especially on unqualified continuation of the one-sided alliance with the United States and regarding relations with Taiwan, China, and the two Koreas.

To a substantial degree Japan's policy toward Asia still takes on meaning in domestic politics in terms of Japanese-American relations. During the past five years two incidents were particularly important in this regard: the Nixon "shocks" of 1971 and the collapse of American policy in Indochina in 1975. The cumulative impact of these events has been to raise questions about the real aims of American policy in Asia and about the capacity (i.e., the will) of the United States to remain strategically engaged in the region. In short, doubt has been raised about American credibility, and this has influenced Japanese politics in several ways.

On the left, the Japanese Socialist Party, while continuing its anti-American rhetoric, has also made cautious efforts to build bridges to Washington, partly it would seem because it perceives a genuine risk that the United States might follow the socialists' advice and "go home." At the same time, the Communist Party has taken a strongly nationalist (and anti-American) stance, a posture that includes opposition to the "American-imposed" Nuclear Nonproliferation Treaty. In the short run, the 1971 rebuffs provided by the secret American diplomatic initiatives toward China and the forced adjustment in bilateral trade relations severely weakened pro-American bureaucrats and conservative party leaders and shocked Japan's international businessmen. The oil crisis, Watergate, and the ignominious collapse of Indochina further affected the conservatives in ways directly con-

nected with Japan's policy toward Asia. The old divisions
among the party politicians (the Taiwan–South Korea
group vs. the China–Asia détente group) persist, but the
lines between them have blurred as Japanese policy moves
pragmatically toward broader contacts with communist
states in Asia *and* at the same time cultivates deeper ties with
noncommunist states (e.g., Indonesia, Korea, Thailand)
through aid, trade, and investment. Japan's more autonomous and complex policies toward East Asia have inevitably
resulted in frequent shifts by conservative leaders on issues
such as China and Korea and in consequence has dragged
these questions into party struggles at a moment when the
internal political situation is in turmoil.

With Japanese ratification of the Nuclear Nonproliferation Treaty in 1976, with Washington's recent stress on
strengthening the alliance, and with the uncertainties in
China over Mao's succession, Japan will probably not move
toward a truly autonomous political-strategic posture in
Asia in the immediate future. However, the trauma and
uncertainties of the last five years have given rise to more
serious consideration of an expanded military role by Japan
in Asia than at any time since 1952. Political stalemate makes
improbable any internally generated move by Japan for a
broadened response to any Asian crisis threatening Japanese
interests. Japan is now sailing on international seas for
which the existing charts are not fully accurate and without
a strong captain in charge. Whether the future of the
Japanese role in Asia is smooth or stormy depends not so
much on the choices of political leaders in Tokyo as on the
winds of change within the region. Over these they have
little control.

Notes

1. It is also interesting to note that by 1976 the Middle East
had replaced the United States as the main trading partner of
the EEC.

2. Although the share of regional trade taken by the
United States dropped slightly, it is really notable that it

remained at the level it has.

3. In 1974 Japan's trade with the oil-producing countries around the Persian Gulf doubled to 15.5 percent of its total trade.

6. Southeast Asia Reexamines Its Options

Guy J. Pauker

The countries of Southeast Asia are currently reassessing their position among themselves, with regard to the major powers that have an impact on their affairs, and in the world at large. They all face a perennial internal crisis due to uneven economic development under conditions of rapid population growth, global inflation, technologically boosted social mobilization, and changing cultural values.

Their relations with the outside world are uncertain and complicated because of changes in the policies of the major powers interested in the region. Concern and suspicion about each others' intentions obstruct cooperative activities among some neighbors and prevent the relaxation of tensions among others.

Relations between the communist governments in control of the Indochinese peninsula and the noncommunist governments of the five member countries of the Association of Southeast Asian Nations (ASEAN) are marked by political hostility and ideological cleavage. This deep polarization within the region is not paralleled by attitudes toward the major external powers. Three ASEAN countries have exchanged diplomatic missions with the People's Republic of China, while Hanoi signals its interest in normalizing relations with the United States, albeit on its own terms. The

international positions of all these countries are not un-
equivocal alignments but complex vectors of power politics,
ideology, economic interests, national pride, security concerns, and the idiosyncrasies of their leaders. The only
possible generalization is that Southeast Asia is not in any
way a homogeneous entity.

Twenty Years Ago and Now

How conditions have changed in the region becomes
apparent by comparing the current international orienta-
tions of Southeast Asian countries with those of twenty years
ago, when after the Geneva Conference of July 1954 and the
Bandung Conference of April 1955 these nations first asserted themselves as independent actors in world affairs.

Thailand, the Philippines, and South Vietnam were
firmly aligned with the West, dependent for their security on
the United States. The territories that later became the
Federation of Malaysia, and Singapore, were also in the
Western camp, through the link of the British Common-
wealth. North Vietnam alone was a communist country,
trying to maintain its distance from the People's Republic of
China—despite the substantial military aid that had contributed to the 1954 victory against the French—while being
curiously neglected during those years by the Soviet Union.
Burma, Indonesia, Laos, and Cambodia professed nonalignment in the global power struggle of the Cold War, although
they maintained close economic and cultural links with
their respective formal colonial overlords and were ideologically closer to the West than to the communist world.

By contrast with the 1950s, a significant shift toward
nonalignment has occurred among the formerly pro-
Western countries. The area controlled by local communist
regimes now encompasses the whole Indochinese peninsula
and provides an expanded arena for some of the bouts of
Sino-Soviet rivalry.

The position of the West has also deteriorated considerably in terms of power politics, although Western economic
involvement has substantially expanded in the noncommu-

nist countries of the region. The industrial democracies also remain the most important source of technology transfer and higher education for the noncommunist countries, while the communist countries of Southeast Asia depend heavily on Soviet, Chinese, and Eastern European sources for similar benefits.

The End of Anglo-American Hegemony

In terms of power politics, by contrast with the 1950s, Great Britain has ceased to have an influential military presence in the region. After reaching the conclusion that its defense forces were "seriously overstretched," the Labour government that came to power in late 1964 set in train a by now completed policy of withdrawal from east of Suez.

In turn, American dominance came to an end following the communist victories in Indochina of April 1975, for which the stage had been set by the proclamation of the Guam Doctrine in July 1969 and by the War Powers Resolution adopted by the Congress in November 1973, both of which reflected widespread opposition in the United States to the Vietnam war and more broadly to all forms of military intervention abroad.

U.S. military forces are still present in the Philippines, although the bases they use are currently subject to renegotiation, but all U.S. bases in Thailand have been closed, and all military personnel have left. The era of Anglo-American hegemony, which resulted from Japan's defeat in 1945, is over. The outline of what the new pattern of power relations will be is not yet discernible.

The Soviets and the Chinese, despite heavy investments in the wars of Indochina, have made only modest advances in terms of establishing their presence in the region in ways that would give them military advantages in the Asian power balance. Consequently it appears that Southeast Asia now experiences less direct military pressure by powers external to the region than at any time since the Portuguese conquest of Malacca in 1511. This is of course what the nationalist elites, these potent antibodies created by the trauma of foreign invasion, have always wanted. Now the countries of Southeast Asia can look forward to a future to be shaped primarily by their own national wills rather than by external forces. The results will be worth watching.

Forsaking Foreign Political Institutions

Concomitantly with the waning of Western dominance, political institutions derived from American, British, Dutch, or French variants of representative government have been abandoned in Southeast Asia by the nationalist elites, which had adopted them with considerable eagerness in the initial period of transition from colonialism to independent national existence.

One should avoid the oversimplified conclusion that those institutions were swept away by the withdrawing Western tide. The constitutional arrangements adopted in the Philippines, Malaysia, Burma, Indonesia, and the non-communist parts of Indochina at the time of independence were discarded because they did not work in indigenous settings.

Whether the survival value of these alien political institutions would have been greater if politico-military Western influences in the region had remained stronger is an interesting question. The much longer historical experience of Latin America suggests a weak correlation between the capacity of the Western democracies to control the foreign relations of developing countries and the lasting implantation of representative government.

The October 1976 coup in Thailand suggests that non-communist Southeast Asia is heading for the same nefarious treadmill from which Latin America has been unable to escape after a century-and-a-half of independence, namely, alternation of civilian and military authoritarian regimes. Communist regimes seem immune to these forms of political instability but are plagued instead by succession crises.

In Southeast Asia it is still premature to appraise developments in the Indochinese peninsula after the great convulsions of 1975. So far, the new communist regimes seem to show little inclination to follow closely the policies of the major communist powers. While acknowledging gratefully the aid received from the Soviet Union during the war, the Lao Dong Party, having proclaimed the Socialist Republic of Vietnam, continues the independent policies it has followed for the last thirty years. The macabre social engineering of the Khmer Rouge has no close analogies in the recent history of the communist world, and the amiable communization underway in Laos seems equally homegrown.

It is tempting to suggest that the only feature common to all Southeast Asian countries, noncommunist as well as communist, is a marked propensity to reject foreign interference in their domestic affairs and the desire to develop autochthonous solutions to their problems.

Southeast Asia Turns Inward

During the first decades of their independent existence, the countries of Southeast Asia were buffeted by forces beyond their control, forces emanating from the major outside powers: pressure to join alliances, overt and covert interference in their internal affairs, economic dependence on a world market over which they had no control and on aid programs with a variety of strings attached, and high-energy cultural penetration.

Now the countries of Southeast Asia seem to be turning away from primary dependence on the major powers, looking inward, seeking practical formulas for self-reliance. Beyond their own region, the countries of Southeast Asia seem to recognize, like other Third World nations, the imperative of closing ranks and strengthening their solidarity in the sharpening North-South confrontation.

The propensity to avoid excessive dependence on major outside powers seems to be requited by the flagging interest of the latter, who appear more concerned with one another than with the smaller nations from among which they previously recruited their clients. What is being played on the wide stage of Asia is a balance-of-power politics, in which context the countries of Southeast Asia are of relatively minor importance, lacking the independent resources without which it is difficult to hold a significant role in the modern version of that play.

Even Vietnam, although it has the largest and most effective military establishment in the region, is logistically too dependent on external sources of support to have a significant impact on broader inter-Asian relations outside Southeast Asia.

Mutual disengagement seems to be the dominant feature shaping relations between the countries of Southeast Asia and the major powers within and outside Asia at this time. But this trend is the result rather than the cause of the specific policies adopted by each government. All face the difficult task of making decisions under conditions of greater uncertainty than in the recent past.

The American Factor

One obvious and fundamental change in the international environment is the changing role of the United States. No country in Southeast Asia is really determining its future course without taking the American factor into account. To the extent that one can generalize on what are essentially judgmental conclusions by Southeast Asian politicians and diplomats of diverse background and outlook, it is still widely assumed that the formidable potential of the United States would be mobilized if the global balance or even the all-Asian equilibrium of forces were in jeopardy. But Southeast Asian governments do not think that the United States would intervene decisively if local insurgencies or interventions from within the region were to threaten their political regimes or even their territorial integrity. Southeast Asian views concerning the credibility of the United States as a guarantor of the status quo have become quite sophisticated: it is assumed that American intervention is most likely to occur in the least likely contingencies, namely, large-scale conflicts among some of the major powers, but is least likely to materialize in the most likely contingencies, such as insurgencies or local armed conflicts between neighboring countries.

Hanoi's Intentions

The most worrisome source of uncertainty in Southeast Asia today concerns the intentions of the Vietnamese leaders. Being in Jakarta in 1975 at the time of the fall of Saigon, I was exposed to the conflicting views of the most experienced Indonesian observers. Some assumed that being communists, the victorious Vietnamese leaders will want to help establish as soon as possible like-minded governments in Thailand, Malaysia, the Philippines, and Indonesia. Others argued that, as nationalists, the Lao Dong hierarchy will want to mobilize all available resources for the economic rehabilitation and development of their country after thirty years of turmoil and violence.

The assumption of the optimists was that the Vietnamese would be prompted to adopt a conciliatory or even cooperative policy toward the noncommunist governments of Southeast Asia, rather than to alarm them, in order to relax tensions in the region and increase their chances to obtain external aid. Vietnam was even encouraged to join ASEAN.

Defying friendly overtures from the ASEAN countries, Hanoi has been broadcasting appeals to all communist underground groups in Southeast Asia to step up their fight to overthrow noncommunist governments. On February 28, 1976, an authoritative editorial in *Nhan Dan* pledged Vietnam's full support to such uprisings, sending cold chills through the ASEAN governments, which had feared since April 1975 that captured American weapons would be made available by the Vietnamese communists to insurgent groups in their countries.

Then, at the first session of the National Assembly of Vietnam, on June 25, 1976, Le Duan, first secretary of the Central Committee of the Lao Dong Party, stated ambiguously in his report that Vietnam's foreign policy will "fully support the just struggle of the people in Southeast Asia for national independence, democracy and social progress," which sounds like an endorsement of revolutionary movements in the region; but he added in the same paragraph that his government was "ready to establish and develop relations of friendship and cooperation with other countries in

Southeast Asia," on the basis of the five principles of coexistence adopted by the 1955 Bandung Conference.

The ambiguity of Hanoi's position was even more evident in the interview given by Vice-Premier and Minister for Foreign Affairs Nguyen Duy Trinh on July 5, before the departure of his deputy Phan Hien for a visit to ASEAN countries. In that interview he stated that "the Vietnamese people fully support the Southeast Asian *peoples'* just cause of national independence, peace, democracy and social progress"; he thus seems to have deliberately refrained from making any promises to the present *governments* of Southeast Asia.

Although in the summer of 1976 Hanoi senior officials visited the capitals of the ASEAN countries and made reassuring statements about their intentions, the governments of countries that had experienced almost thirty years of subversive activities organized by the communist underground in their respective countries remained skeptical about the value of these Lao Dong assurances.

In October 1976, after an authoritarian regime was established in Thailand following violent clashes between right-wing and left-wing students, large-scale security operations were staged against communist and other leftist elements, discarding in the process any pretense of peaceful coexistence between Thailand and its communist neighbors.

The Unpredictable Major Powers

Another source of uncertainty confronting the governments of Southeast Asia concerns the interplay between the major powers external to the region who have a determinant role in its affairs, namely, the United States, the Soviet Union, China, and Japan.

For the United States, Southeast Asia has become a low-priority area compared with the Middle East and southern Africa, after a lengthy period during which the governments of the region had been led to believe that their orientation was considered of major importance from the point of view of American interests. In the capitals of Southeast Asia, the political and strategic downgrading of their countries is still not fully understood, and the longer-term implications have not yet been worked out.

The Soviet Union, despite its manifest interest in maintaining some presence in the region and in the Indian Ocean, has been less aggressive in its forward movement than was expected after the communist victories in Indochina. Contrary to earlier speculations, it has not devoted large material resources for the purpose of replacing the vanishing American presence. It has acquired no base rights or other facilities on the coast of Vietnam and has made no visible progress, if it had intended to do so, toward forging an anti-Chinese coalition.

The apparent victory of moderate elements in the People's Republic of China in October 1976, very shortly after the death of Mao Tse-tung, makes it unlikely that a vigorous policy of revolutionary subversion will be pursued against the ASEAN countries. On the contrary, China is likely to prefer the status quo, which facilitates the gradual neutralization of the region, to political-military adventures that would risk the renewed involvement of the United States and might give the Soviet Union opportunities it now seems to lack.

Japan, facing an election in an atmosphere of scandals that has eroded the political strength of the dominant Liberal-Democratic Party, is perhaps the greatest factor of uncertainty at this time. For the first time since the end of World War II, the emergence of a new governmental coalition is a likely possibility. The foreign policy orientation of such a government might be even more cautious than previous Japanese governments have been in recent decades.

As Japan is today the only major power with very substantial interests in Southeast Asia, such a development might curtail even further the region's capacity to maneuver in the global arena. During the past decade American policymakers have occasionally entertained the idea that Japan

could in the future assume some of the security responsibilities in Southeast Asia relinquished by the United States. The
likelihood that Japan would accept that role has always been
slim. It would vanish altogether if neutralist elements enter
the cabinet.

These political uncertainties are compounded by old and
new economic problems. The major powers with free market
economies have still not fully overcome the crises of the
recent past. Economic aid is only reluctantly continued,
even at levels substantially below the 0.7 percent of GNP
pledged at the beginning of the United Nations Second
Development Decade in 1970. Private foreign investments
are sluggish, in part because of the visible ascendancy of
radical nationalist trends in most ASEAN countries.

The United States and Japan, as well as most countries of
the European Economic Community, are still fighting
inflation, have high unemployment rates, and face the
complex international economic problems created by fluc-
tuating currencies. Under prevailing circumstances, the best
that the ASEAN countries can expect is that governmental
economic aid and private foreign investments from the
industrial democracies will not drop substantially below the
level of the last decade. The communist countries of Indochina can at best expect token contributions from the same
sources.

The Arab oil-exporting countries, which have enormous
surpluses of investment capital and a relatively low domestic
absorptive capacity, are viewed by the ASEAN countries as
potentially a major new source of economic aid, besides the
industrial democracies and international financial institutions controlled by the West, such as the World Bank and the
International Monetary Fund. But although the Arab countries are acquiring experience and gaining self-confidence in
the making of investment decisions, the total flow of capital
from the Middle East to Southeast Asia is still a modest
fraction of felt needs.

The communist powers do not show much promise either.
The Soviet Union, although it acts like an ambitious and

assertive global power, gives no indication of planning to expand its role in Southeast Asia significantly, with the possible exception of Vietnam, which is allegedly receiving about $500 million worth of economic assistance annually. The absence of major Soviet aid programs in Southeast Asia is not surprising. Although it might be tempted to outclass the United States at this time, the Soviet government faces perennial agricultural uncertainties, while it must also intensify capital formation and respond to increasing domestic demand for consumer goods. At the same time it wants to keep up the strategic competition with the United States in the nuclear field and exploit various targets of opportunity in other parts of the Third World. The Soviet Union is not likely to assume major financial burdens in the form of substantial credits to the noncommunist countries of Southeast Asia. Its trade with the region is slowly expanding, but unless the Soviet Union is prepared to play a major role in the area, its influence will not grow much in those credit-hungry and growth-anxious countries.

As for the People's Republic of China, in the past it has had little to offer the countries of Southeast Asia. Unlike the United States, Japan, and to a lesser, but still significant degree, the Soviet Union, the People's Republic of China has not been and will not be for some time a significant source of technology transfer, investment capital, or commercial credits. Its present influence in the area results primarily from the eagerness of vulnerable Southeast Asian governments to appease the Peking government, which they see as a potential source of support to local insurgents. Trade with the People's Republic of China, as with the Soviet Union, has been insignificant compared with trade with the United States, Japan, and Western Europe. It is not even clear whether China will become an important exporter of oil. If it does, it may become an interesting source of supply to some countries of Southeast Asia, such as Thailand and the Philippines, but also a worrisome competitor to Indonesia, especially in the Japanese market. But whether China's growing oil production and its increasing capacity to export grains will become sources of enhanced leverage in Southeast Asia will depend primarily on Peking's willingness to grant commercial credits rather than demand cash payments in foreign exchange, which is much needed for China's own development-related imports.

To recapitulate, none of the major powers seems eager at this time to increase substantially their political and economic involvement in the affairs of Southeast Asia. The only possible exception is the Soviet Union. If its future relations with the Socialist Republic of Vietnam are driven by ambitious strategic interests, we may still witness a massive Soviet involvement in that country. But it is important to remember that in the last two decades all major powers, without exception, have experienced the volatility of the Southeast Asian situation.

No country in the region has proved to be in the long run a reliable political ally or economic partner, and no commitments have been immune to sudden reversals. All the major powers have reason to be cautious in their future dealing in this high-risk region. Consequently, the countries of Southeast Asia may find their opportunities to play off one major power against another drastically curtailed, which will reduce their diplomatic flexibility and increase the uncertainties under which they have to operate in the international arena.

The North-South Conflict

Another consequential source of uncertainty results from the fact that regardless of their specific economic interests with regard to the price of oil, metals, or tropical agricultural products, or concerning the treatment of multinational corporations and other external sources of private capital, technology transfer, and management skills, the noncommunist countries of Southeast Asia are under considerable moral and political pressure, as members of the Third World, to close ranks and present a united front in the North-South confrontation with the industrial democracies.

Although investment decisions are not made in the normal course of events in response to the rhetoric used at the United Nations or at special gatherings in Algiers or Paris, the cumulative effect of the North-South confrontation is to erode gradually the climate of confidence that in the past attracted private foreign investments to Southeast Asia.

National elites that want to avoid "Maoist" patterns of development, controlled by parties of mass-mobilization dedicated to radical social transformations, are facing an obvious dilemma, the implications of which may not yet be fully comprehended in the countries of Southeast Asia. They are dependent on transfers of capital and technology from the West and Japan for the achievement of their economic growth plans. But such cooperative endeavors between developed and developing countries may be seriously jeopardized if the North-South confrontation is exacerbated, especially at at time when the economic difficulties confronting the United States, Japan, and Western Europe inhibit their interest in an area of relatively minor importance as a supplier of natural resources, as a market for industrial products, and as an arena for the investment of venture capital. Only when the global economy is in a period of expansion does Southeast Asia really appear attractive to foreign investors. When retrenchment sets in, requiring a sober assessment of priorities, Southeast Asia does not rate very highly.

Now the region's potential for political instability has been enhanced by the communist victories in Indochina. Added to the growing malaise created by the increasing militancy of the Third World's demands for a New International Economic Order, this situation results in a marked erosion of the climate of confidence that in the past decade brought relatively large amounts of private foreign capital into Southeast Asia.

Obstacles to Intraregional Cooperation

The communist states of Southeast Asia face in many ways similar uncertainties in a world in which relations between the major powers are in flux and in which the pressing issues of economic development are difficult to handle by countries poor in natural resources and trained manpower. But the antagonistic relations between communist and noncommunist Southeast Asian countries make generalizations across the ideological divide excessively tenuous.

The members of ASEAN, the communist states, and isolationist Burma are not likely to make common cause on any important issue, be it an adversary relation with some of the major external powers or active cooperation within the region. Although all these countries seem to be turning inward, the result is not increased solidarity within the region, but fragmentation in the guise of affirmation of separate national identities.

The reality of this trend was verified by the first summit meeting held by ASEAN in February 1976 in Bali. Established in August 1967 to promote economic and cultural cooperation among its members, ASEAN has become a forum for regular consultations among the foreign ministers of the five member countries and has provided an institutional framework for consultations between working-level officials. But it made little headway in accelerating economic growth in the region which was the first objective of the ASEAN declaration, although concrete proposals of considerable merit had been prepared by UN experts in 1973.

The Bali meeting brought the five heads of government together for the first time eight-and-a-half years after the adoption of the ASEAN declaration in Bangkok. Despite the common perception of an enhanced threat to their regimes following the communist victories in Indochina, no steps were taken to turn ASEAN into a multilateral security organization or to adopt some other kind of joint approach to defense. The opposition came from Malaysia, which, although threatened by a resumption of the communist insurgency that had plagued it for many years, is anxious not to provoke its communist neighbors on the Indochinese peninsula. Security cooperation among ASEAN countries will therefore continue on an ad hoc bilateral basis.

No "Zone of Neutrality"

Although Southeast Asia is divided into two groups of countries that are at least ideologically adversary, Malaysia also insisted that ASEAN must remain "nonideological, nonmilitary, nonantagonistic" and continued to advance the idea that Southeast Asia should become a "zone of peace, freedom, and neutrality," which the ASEAN foreign ministers had politely endorsed in their Kuala Lumpur declaration of November 1971. At the Bali summit the heads of government apparently agreed that the zone of neutrality idea had merit but would not be worth pursuing until the three communist states of Indochina responded favorably to the invitation to join ASEAN, which some ASEAN leaders believe possible, despite Hanoi's explicit acts of hostility at the present time.

When the late Malaysian prime minister Tun Abdul Razak first voiced this idea at the Third Nonaligned Summit Conference at Lusaka in September 1970, the purpose was to promote a "hands off" policy by the major powers external to the region. At that time the United States had half a million combat forces in Vietnam and considerable air and naval forces deployed in Southeast Asia, while the Soviet Union and the People's Republic of China were providing massive military resources to the communist forces in Indochina.

Neutralization was seen at the time by Malaysia as a process in two stages, involving first an agreement among the countries in the region on ways of ensuring peace among themselves and then an agreement among the major powers external to the region to respect and guarantee the neutrality of Southeast Asia. The underlying idea was that the region could be excluded from the Asian power balance if it ceased being an arena for great-power competition.

Paradoxically, although involvement of the great powers in the region has diminished, chances for neutralization either by international agreement or through a unilateral declaration by the countries of Southeast Asia seem less favorable than six years ago. At present, the Sino-Soviet

competition is one of the most dynamic features of the
diplomatic life in the capitals of Southeast Asia. The notion
that Moscow and Peking, under current assumptions, would
join in a "hands off" agreement on Southeast Asia is unrealistic.

Besides, as long as the Soviet Union asserts uninhibited
global ambitions on the high seas and in the Third World,
the United States is not likely to abandon its present Pacific
strategy, which involves the forward deployment of naval
and air forces in the Philippines. Active American cooperation in a neutralization scheme for Southeast Asia would
require, as a prerequisite, unambiguous manifestation of
Soviet intentions to exercise global self-restraint, not just
ritualistic invocations of détente.

But the most serious obstacle to the neutralization of
Southeast Asia is the situation created by the antagonism
between the ASEAN countries and the communist regimes
in Indochina. Hanoi's aggressive propaganda against
ASEAN and its member governments, and the call to arms
and promise of support it has addressed to all communist
undergrounds in the region are hardly an auspicious setting
for a policy for neutralization, the essence of which is
noninterference and renunciation of violence. Equally un-
promising are the repressive anticommunist policies
pursued by the ASEAN governments. This ideological
cleavage is not likely to be overcome unless drastic changes
of regime occur in one or both camps.

No ASEAN Free Trade Area

ASEAN is also not yet ready to play an important role in
Asian affairs as a collective economic entity. This was
demonstrated by the failure of the Bali summit meeting to
agree on a free trade area, which Singapore, supported by the
Philippines, advocated and Indonesia rejected after lengthy
preliminary negotiations in the fall of 1975. Prime Minister
Lee Kuan Yew of Singapore commented in a resigned mood
at the opening of the Bali summit that "new nations need
time to realize that sovereignty does not mean self-

sufficiency." But it behooved the new prime minister of Malaysia, Datuk Hussein Onn, to grasp the essence of what regionalism is at this stage in the development of the nations of Southeast Asia: "ASEAN exists," he said, "because it serves a need. It continues to exist because it does not demand from us what we cannot give." Although agreement has since been reached on a number of industrial joint ventures destined to assist all five countries, it will take years before these projects materialize and even longer before they have an impact on the relations of the five countries among themselves and with the rest of the world.

In searching for new options in the unpredictable international environment of the last quarter of this century, the nations of Southeast Asia will not have an easy time of it. Their strategic location at the crossroads of continents and oceans precludes isolation. They will remain vulnerable to the thrusts of great power competition. They will also be buffeted by growing internal and regional tensions generated by their own intransigent nationalism, economic backwardness, and social inequity. On the political weather map of the Pacific Basin, Southeast Asia will remain for many years to come a low-pressure area, from which one can expect storm more often than sunshine.

7. India's Asian Relations

Richard L. Park

Jawaharlal Nehru made it clear from the early days of independence that India considered itself an important middle power with aspirations for major-power status. Neighboring Asian countries warranted special attention, but the nation's perspectives were worldwide not regional. Mr. Nehru's speech on foreign policy of September 26, 1946, included this summary:

> It is necessary that, with the attainment of her full international status, India should establish contact with all the great nations of the world and that her relations with neighboring countries in Asia should become still closer.[1]

The history of India's foreign and international economic policies since 1947 bear out the fact that the government of India has pursued external policies of significance in many parts of the world. Indeed, a case can be made that Western and Eastern Europe, the USSR, North America, the Middle East, and Africa received greater emphasis than Asia, the exceptions being critical and continuing problems with other South Asian countries and China. If much of the rest of the world considered India poor, overpopulated, and

underdeveloped—in effect, a country unable to fulfill commitments to its own people, much less to others abroad—the
leaders of India have persisted in projecting a more all-
encompassing image of its role in world affairs. Jawaharlal
Nehru, to his death in 1964, was able to maintain a large
measure of influence in the United Nations, as a leader of the
nonaligned bloc, and in contributing to the shaping of
international economic and security policies because of his
personal international standing. Those who succeeded him
in the prime ministership have not been as successful,
although the Nehru momentum has not been entirely lost.

The defeat of Indira Gandhi and her ruling Congress
Party in the parliamentary elections of March 1977 will not
result in major shifts in foreign policy under the winning
Janata (People's) Party, headed by Prime Minister Morarji
Desai. Indeed, one of the first major addresses by the new
minister of external affairs, Mr. Atal Bihari Vajpayee, on
March 30, 1977, stressed the continuities that would charac-
terize the government's approaches in world affairs.
Changes there will be, especially to manage nonalignment
in a more balanced way. But fundamental alterations in
strategy are not to be expected, at least in the short run.

It is crucial to appreciate that India, like Japan, the
People's Republic of China, the USSR, the United States,
and the major West European countries, holds a world view
that is global. Current domestic policies are directed toward
achieving self-sufficiency to avoid external influences
brought on by economic or military dependency. Criticisms
of the United States and China in the past made reference to
policies that would restrict India from reaching its ambitions of becoming a major power. American and Chinese
decisions to favor Pakistan in the Bangladesh war of 1971
were cases in point.

Others tend to see India as a country that should concentrate its efforts and limited resources on the development of
its own economy, building constructive and friendly contacts with immediate neighbors, and working cooperatively
with smaller Asian nations toward greater political stability,

reduced sources of potential conflict, and increased regional security. Such goals are not outside the range of the country's policies, but India also wants to help assure peace everywhere; to rearrange existing trade, banking, shipping, and import-export patterns that impede development in the poorer parts of the world; and to assert the rights of the many over the privileges of the few by creating a world order where the interests of the majority are given appropriate weight.

The essentials of India's external and domestic political strategies cannot be grasped without understanding these broader goals, however unrealistic they may seem to be at the present time. They in part explain why India's standing defense force numbers over one million and why direct defense costs exceed 26 percent of annual governmental expenditures, despite recurrent internal economic crises. The underground testing of a nuclear device in 1974 is another relevant example. As far as security is concerned, India realizes that no country—certainly not the United States or the Soviet Union—would risk the dangers of nuclear war at home to come to India's rescue in times of emergency; outsiders would think twice even in providing conventional military assistance. If one aspires to independence of action and influence abroad, there is no alternative: India also must be a nuclear power. Similarly, if economic dependence, and thus potential restrictions on external influence, is induced by food and petroleum imports, for example, then maximum self-sufficiency in these areas must be among the national targets. Also, if relations with countries in Asia are unambiguously in India's interests, short-term or longer, then they should be developed; otherwise they should not. India's Asia policy fits within a larger framework, but it is not necessarily at its center.

Students of India's foreign policy have reviewed the record since 1947 in numerous studies.[2] This analysis is confined to recent developments and future trends in intra-Asian policies. Today's and tomorrow's decisions, however, rest upon a background of experience, domestic and foreign, that should be outlined briefly.

1. India existed as a part of Great Britain's imperial system for two hundred years. Independence was gained only thirty years ago, after the growth of a nationalist movement that boosted selfconfidence in the latter years, but that also ended in a partition of the subcontinent, widespread violence, destruction, and the displacement of over 12 million people. As of 1947, the economy was largely undeveloped and its industrial sector consumer-based; the economy was further broken by the political division of the subcontinent and was burdened by millions of refugees, rising unemployment, inadequate housing, poor sources of energy, and transportation and communications systems deteriorated by heavy use in World War II. India's memory of its colonial past and the horrors that accompanied the achievement of independence were bitter then, and remain so.

2. India in 1977 is a country of about 630 million people, growing at the rate of approximately 2.4 percent each year, which currently means that nearly 14 million are added to the population annually. The production of food grains in 1977, assuming satisfactory monsoons, will reach or exceed 120 million tons; industrial production, housing, employment, literacy, and education are expanding. But specific targets in these fields often are not met, demands for a better life increase, and the political system is overloaded with pressures for support from every side: the rising population inexorably pushes these difficult conditions to the edges of crises. Thus domestic policies must receive first priority—now and for the foreseeable future.

3. The Indian political system is unstable and unbalanced. The Emergency of 1975 was a dramatic reflection of this condition.[3] Effective external policies stem from internal stability, a sense of security, and a popular consensus on the proper working of the governmental apparatus. Such circumstances are unlikely to be present in India for some years to come, although the government of Morarji Desai since March 1977 has made major strides in restoring normalcy following the end of the Emergency.

4. India is the dominant political power in South Asia

and has been since 1947. The country is, in this sense, a potential "imperialist" power in the eyes of smaller, nearby countries. Relations with its immediate neighbors have been troubled, and that condition continues.

5. India has fought four wars in thirty years of independence: 1947-1948, 1965, and 1971 with Pakistan; 1962 with the People's Republic of China. The costs—in manpower, finances, morale, and security—have been great.

6. The Sino-Soviet dispute hovers over the subcontinent.[4] India chose in 1971 to seek a treaty of friendship with the USSR,[5] resulting in China's further irritation toward India and its increased attention to Pakistan and more recently to Bangladesh. As India now moves to improve diplomatic contacts with China, the Soviet Union has become more tentative about what priority to give to Indo-Soviet cooperation.

7. India, with Egypt and Yugoslavia, gave initial form to the nonaligned world, and it continues to be an important member of that bloc, including the "Group of 77" in the General Assembly. Domestic concerns and competition for leadership among the nonaligned, however, have reduced the centrality of India's role.

8. India has committed itself to be nuclear power.[6] The immediate benefits appear to be small, and the cost high. The nuclear genie is out of the bottle in the subcontinent. Pakistan intends to respond with parallel developments and is setting out to accomplish these ends.

9. Finally, India has less reason to address the world on the greater strength of moral over physical power. For the most part, India has opted for the traditional elements of physical power, and it is outweighed by the major players in this deadly game.

Economic Overview

Trade patterns do not coincide perfectly with national interests, but they are positive indicators. Trade is bound to have an impact on foreign policy. The following table shows India's imports and exports from 1970 through 1974.[7] The figures delineate sharply that India does most of its business abroad with the United States, the United Kingdom, West Germany, the USSR, and Japan. In the case of Iran, exports to India are mostly oil. The high level of exports from India to Bangladesh in 1972-1973 arose as a result of special circumstances: the dire need for food and other daily necessities in Bangladesh following its successful war for independence from Pakistan in 1971. In 1976, trade between India and the USSR totaled one billion dollars. Overall, it can be seen that Indian trade (both imports and exports) with Asia has been modest, with the exception of Japan. More recent evidence indicates no major change in this basic trade pattern.

The fact is that India does not have a complementary economic balance with most of Asia. In the case of Japan, on the other hand, most of India's exports are iron ore, coal, and other raw materials needed by the Japanese industrial complex, and Indian imports from Japan have been machinery, spare parts, special forms of steel for use in industrial construction, and sophisticated instruments for control over industrial production standards. We conclude that, at least at present, commerce is unlikely to be an important tie between India and most of the rest of Asia, except for certain commodities and at low annual levels of exchange.

Since the Arab-Israeli war of 1973 and the precipitate and major rise in the cost of oil and petroleum products, the Indian economy has been hit hard, probably harder than any other single country in the developing world. For example, the cost of imported oil and petroleum products in 1971-1972 was $266 million, whereas in 1975-1976 the cost of the same products was $1,710 million. It is expected that for 1976-1977, the import need of India will be at least 13.5 million tons of oil and 2.1 million tons of petroleum products, at a total cost of $1,786 million. Most of these products come from Iran, Iraq, the United Arab Emirates, and Saudi Arabia. Oil and petroleum products, of course, are needed not only for their direct use as energy, but also in the production of fertilizers and pharmaceuticals. Contrasted

INDIA'S IMPORTS AND EXPORTS (1970-71 to 1973-74)[a]
(Selected countries. Figures given in lakhs[b] of rupees.)

Country	1970-71 Imports	1970-71 Exports	1971-72 Imports	1971-72 Exports	1972-73 Imports	1972-73 Exports	1973-74 Imports	1973-74 Exports
USA	45,295	20,734	41,869	26,308	23,487	27,574	49,341	34,278
UK	12,676	17,044	22,031	16,870	23,725	17,253	24,481	25,839
Germany (West)	10,747	5,231	12,704	3,710	17,258	6,228	19,573	8,225
Iran	9,164	(c)	12,636	(c)	12,198	(c)	26,758	(c)
Japan	8,343	20,348	15,160	18,227	17,853	21,716	25,557	35,513
USSR	10,613	20,985	8,732	20,870	11,437	30,482	24,975	28,379
Malaysia	575	1,173	385	1,173	842	934	3,209	2,408
Bangladesh	---	---	(c)	4,279	346	16,824	1,689	5,873
Burma	964	1,403	587	1,078	205	436	7	154
Singapore	117	1,763	295	1,760	283	1,784	971	4,293
Sri Lanka	(c)	3,182	(c)	2,124	(c)	801	(c)	979
Indonesia	(c)	410	(c)	321	(c)	530	(c)	2,675
Total for all countries[d]	163,420	153,516	182,45-	160,822	186,744	197,083	292,091	248,322

[a]Source: India: A Reference Annual, 1976, New Delhi: Government of India, 1976), pp. 297-299.

[b]One lakh equals 100,000.

[c]Figures not given; negligible or small amounts.

[d]Totals include all selected countries given in the table, as well as other countries not listed.

with the petroleum needs of India, the indigenous production is totally inadequate, despite some increases in local
production since independence. Local oil production for
1976-1977, for example, is estimated to be not more than 9
million tons, and this expectation may not be met.[8]

The oil issue is given some attention because it helps to
explain why trade with the Middle East has become so
critical in the shaping of India's international economic
patterns. It also provides a rationale—in part—for India's
strong support of the Arab world in the Arab-Israeli dispute,
beyond India's reading of the intrinsic merits of the case. The
fact that India had a Muslim population of over 40 million
in 1947 and that the Muslim population exceeds 61 million
in 1977 also adds relevance to the reasoning underlying
India's Middle East policy.

It is conceivable, if relations with the People's Republic of
China improve in the future, that India might be able to
import some of its oil from China out of the massive oil
reserves discovered there in recent years. This notion, however, is pure speculation at this point.

There has been an improvement in the balance of India's
payments from 1976, and foreign exchange reserves reached
a record $2.7 billion in September 1976. These advances,
however, were obtained mostly from trade with parts of the
world other than Asia.[9]

India linked itself politically and psychologically to the
countries of Asia in building affirmative attitudes toward
nonalignment with the power blocs—both the West and the
communist countries—in the years since independence. At
the Bandung Conference in 1955, India played a leading role
side by side with China. India's diplomatic representatives
throughout Asia have encouraged cultural, educational,
political, and some commercial transactions, but domestic
concerns have induced India to turn elsewhere for its international business. Japan's intentions were suspect until
recent years; increased trade and personal relationships have
tended to break down older prejudices.

South Asia

The most active sector of India's external policy has been with its immediate neighbors in South Asia. As was pointed out earlier, the dominant position of India in the subcontinent has been a source of continuing antagonism. India's outlook on national security happens to impinge upon the northern countries—from Afghanistan and Pakistan through Nepal, Bhutan, and Bangladesh. Sri Lanka, although not of immediate security concern to India, is a Bay of Bengal–Indian Ocean country whose importance for security increases because of Soviet and U.S. naval strategies in the area. In addition, Sri Lanka, like the other countries bordering India, has social problems involving Indian subjects (or former Indian subjects) who seek the protection of India in times of local conflict.

Burma, although a part of Southeast Asia, nevertheless borders with India and thus is also of interest in India's security strategies. Relations with Burma have not played any significant role in India's foreign policy since the earliest days of independence, when U Nu and Jawaharlal Nehru managed to keep close personal friendships. With the accession of Ne Win to power, Burma has receded into self-imposed isolation, and Indian ties have declined.

Afghanistan

Afghanistan does not consider itself a part of South Asia; it insists that it is a Middle Eastern country that conducts regular contacts with South Asia mostly because of the need to import goods for Kabul through the port of Karachi in Pakistan.[10] Diplomatic and cultural links with India have been encouraged more for tactical reasons, to take advantage of the conflicts between Pakistan and Afghanistan, than for measurable important mutual interests other than historical friendships first laid in the nationalist period.

It is likely that Afghanistan and Pakistan will make serious efforts to reduce their mutual antagonisms as part of a general pattern of consolidation within the Islamic world.

The president of Afghanistan, General Daoud, who seized power in July 1973, abolished the monarchy, established a republic, and was visited by Prime Minister Bhutto of Pakistan in June 1976. Daoud then visited Islamabad in August of the same year. There is reason to believe that the Shah of Iran was instrumental in bringing about these visits. The disruptive political conditions following the Pakistani elections of early March 1977 have jeopardized Zulfikar Ali Bhutto's power and have reduced the amity between Pakistan and Afghanistan because of uprisings against Bhutto in Baluchistan and the North-West Frontier Province, territories bordering on Afghanistan. It is nevertheless probable that Indo-Afghan priorities in foreign policy will decline as Pakistan and Afghanistan find ways to settle their differences over the next several years.

Pakistan

The circumstances surrounding partition in 1947 made certain that India and Pakistan would be at loggerheads for a long time to come. The two countries have fought three wars, including one in 1971 that was most devastating for Pakistan: supported by India and the Indian army, East Pakistan broke away and became Bangladesh. The issue of Jammu and Kashmir remains a major stumbling block to accord between India and Pakistan, even though in other respects efforts have been made to resolve differences.

Indira Gandhi and Zulfikar Ali Bhutto met in Simla in 1972, reaching an agreement on July 3 to make efforts to normalize relations. It was agreed at Simla that the Kashmir issue would be taken up at a later date. Only modest progress to achieve the goals of the Simla agreement was made before 1976. In that year, Pakistan and India again opened official relationships by exchanging ambassadors, fortuitously or by plan just before the opening of the conference of the non-aligned countries in Colombo. Since 1976, considerable advance has been made in opening road, rail, and air linkages between the two countries, and overflights of one country by aircraft of the other have been approved. Trade also has begun again at limited levels. It appears that India has been somewhat more liberal in granting visas to persons from Pakistan wishing to visit India than Pakistan has been the other way, but the record shows that personal and commercial exchange will increase, slowly but perceptibly.[11]

As far as security is concerned, both India and Pakistan see the other party as a potential adversary. Since India now possesses nuclear power status, Pakistan is negotiating to buy a $150 million nuclear-waste reprocessing plant from France. Canada has terminated its agreement to cooperate in nuclear developments with Pakistan, but discussions continue to reverse this decision. Pakistan also is negotiating to buy 110 A-7 fighter-bombers, and Saudi Arabia has indicated its willingness to finance the sale. The negotiation has been complicated by opposition from the United States to the purchase of the planes, unless Pakistan drops its interest in the French nuclear arrangement noted above.[12]

It is natural for India and Pakistan to develop improved economic and personal relationships because of their contiguity, but Pakistan's longer-range strategies lie with the Islamic world to the west. The twelve-year-old Regional Cooperation for Development, involving Iran, Pakistan, and Turkey, was given more formal status on March 12, 1977, when the foreign ministers of the three countries signed the Treaty of Izmir.[13] The purpose of the treaty is to extend economic, technical, and cultural relations among these three non-Arab Islamic countries, with the expectation of building a free trade zone in this region over the next ten years. The treaty includes clauses calling for the formation of an investment and development bank, an institute of science and technology in Iran, a school of economics and a science foundation in Pakistan, and a youth foundation, as well as a tourism and hotel management school, in Turkey.

India's involvements with Pakistan may decrease as the Islamic world policy of Pakistan grows stronger. Even now, many Pakistanis, both professionals and those less skilled, are engaged in development projects in Saudi Arabia, Kuwait, the United Arab Emirates, and to a lesser extent in Iran.

The special relations between Pakistan and Iran, and the dominant force of the Shah of Iran in this regional development, are suggested by meetings in 1976 between Bhutto and the Shah in March, April, July, and December. Among other Islamic rulers, King Khalid of Saudi Arabia visited Pakistan in October 1976, presented a $30 million gift to Pakistan, and confirmed the availability of interest-free loans.[14]

The economic base of Pakistan's shift to the Islamic world may be seen in Pakistan's balance of payment deficits in 1976 of over $1.5 million. These deficits have been made up by loans of $750 million from the Aid-to-Pakistan Consortium—mostly Western countries—but also by $500 million from the OPEC countries (mostly Iran) and $365 million in remittances from Pakistanis living abroad.

Despite the 1971 loss of Bangladesh and what appeared to be a long period ahead of antagonistic contacts between Bangladesh and Pakistan, Bangladesh more recently has initiated friendly links with Pakistan at the same time that Bangladesh's relations with India have deteriorated. An ambassador from Bangladesh to Pakistan arrived in Islamabad in January 1976, and trade and shipping agreements between the two countries were signed in April of the same year.

Bangladesh

India believed that a free Bangladesh, assisted in its liberation both militarily and economically by India, would remain on friendly terms.[15] This expectation was unrealistic. Traditional rivalries between East Bengal and India—religious, economic, political, and cultural—arose almost immediately after Bangladesh's liberation. The assassination of Sheikh Mujibur Rahman in August 1975 and the murders of many of Mujibur Rahman's associates at the same time or shortly afterwards led to the accession of General Ziaur Rahman in November 1975. Mujibur Rahman was grateful to India for its assistance in bringing Bangladesh into being. But the current regime finds that India is exploitative economically and all too willing to bring its national weight to bear against poverty-stricken, militarily impotent Bangladesh. One of the critical current problems separating the two countries is India's construction of the Farakka Barrage in Indian territory near Bangladesh; this would apparently have the consequence of reducing water supplies for agriculture in Bangladesh. Opposition to the Farakka Barrage was supported by the Islamic Foreign Ministers' Conference in Istanbul in May 1976 and also by a majority attending the 85-nation non-aligned summit conference in Colombo in August 1976. The issue has now been accepted as an agenda item by the General Assembly of the United Nations—against the strong objections of India. In the meantime, India and Bangladesh reached an understanding in April 1977 on the principles that should determine the distribution of water from the barrage. The New Delhi negotiation was conducted by India's Defense Minister, Mr. Jagjivan Ram, and Bangladesh's Chief Martial Law Administrator, General Ziaur Rahman. Thus debate in the United Nations may prove to be unnecessary.

Bangladesh has not been favorably inclined toward India and has turned to Pakistan and the Islamic world (and with caution to the People's Republic of China) for support against what Bangladesh believes are India's pressures for control over Bangladesh. The Desai government in New Delhi is trying to reverse these trends.

Nepal

India's relations with Nepal are complicated by several obvious factors of geography.[16] Nepal is a land-locked country that borders on China to its north and India to its south; for the maintenance of its economy, Nepal must continue close contacts with India. To cite one set of figures, in 1969-1970, 99.16 percent of Nepal's exports went to India, and 99.62 percent of Nepal's imports came from India. These percentages rise and fall somewhat over the years, but the basic balance heavily in favor of India remains stable.

Nepal has been, and continues to be, a classical buffer

state, much as has Afghanistan. Nepal's position has been especially sensitive, however, because of the unfriendly relations between China and India since the border war of 1962. Added to this factor is India's military strategy, which considers Nepal and Bhutan as parts of its northern defense system. Nepalese leaders were again alerted to their special Indian connections when the semiautonomous state of Sikkim lost its unique status in 1974 and was fully absorbed into the territory of India. Nepal's King Birendra and his advisers would prefer that Nepal be considered a "zone of peace" and that Indian influences would decrease substantially. This is unlikely to occur unless India's ties to China improve greatly over the coming years.

Bhutan

Bhutan does not figure in any major way in international affairs, except by virtue of its crucial location on the borders of China and India, much as is the case with Nepal. Although Bhutan and Nepal are members of the United Nations, a special treaty relationship with India requires Bhutan to consult with India on major matters concerning foreign affairs. Bhutan is dependent on India for its import as well as its export markets. There are no alternatives. The fact that the monarchy of Bhutan has been able to maintain some independence of action is to be credited to the skillful political maneuvering of the royal family and its advisers.

Sri Lanka

Sri Lanka is not a high-priority factor in India's South Asian policy, except to the extent of a minor segment of trade, relatively frequent travel between Colombo and the south of India, and cooperation as fellow nonaligned countries.[17] Some irritation has existed between the two since 1947-1948 because of the difficulties encountered by the Tamil-speaking minority in Sri Lanka, who hold ethnic ties to the State of Tamilnadu in south India. Jawaharlal Nehru and Indira Gandhi both negotiated with Sri Lanka for a reduction in tensions between the Tamil-speaking Hindu minority and the Sinhala-speaking Buddhist majority with some success, but the problem is not as yet fully resolved. One other source of conflict, namely, the maritime boundaries between Sri Lanka and India, was resolved in agreements signed in 1976. The Fifth Conference of Heads of State or Government of Nonaligned Countries, held in Colombo in August 1976, was attended by a large Indian delegation, headed by Indira Gandhi. Prime Minister Gandhi gave recognition to the special role played by Sri Lanka as a mediator in the nonaligned world.

Sri Lanka will remain a cooperative associate of India over the coming years and will be looked upon as a place where serious problems separating countries in the Asian world may be discussed. Sri Lanka also may be expected to be a major spokesman for keeping the Indian Ocean area a "zone of peace" in an attempt to restrain Soviet-U.S. naval rivalries in that region.

Southeast Asia

Early statements by students of India's foreign policy concluded that India would make special efforts to build constructive, lasting and deep connections with the countries of Southeast Asia, particularly with Indonesia and countries on the Bay of Bengal—from Burma to Singapore.[18] The special attention India gave to Indonesia in its search for independence from the Netherlands was one case in point; at a later stage, India was one of the first to recognize the People's Republic of China and to encourage the Southeast Asian countries to adjust to the new conditions brought about by Mao Tse-tung's capture of power in China. At a still later stage, India strongly opposed the military intervention by the United States in the second Indochinese war.

Two major factors inhibited the growth of an effective Southeast Asian policy by India. The first was Jawaharlal Nehru's rejection of the idea that India should attempt such a policy. He considered efforts at attaining special status in Southeast Asia a form of interference that would be resented. Nehru believed that the security interests of India required a

detailed concern with India's immediate neighbors in South
Asia, but that the same security argument could not be
extended to Southeast Asia. Furthermore, India's limited
resources and the priority of domestic economic development made it impractical to consider a developmental role in
Southeast Asia in anything more than symbolic ways.

The second obstacle to an active Indian Southeast Asian
policy was the rise during the Cold War of the containment
policy of the United States. This policy resulted not only in a
defense agreement between the United States and Pakistan in
1954, but also in the establishment of the Southeast Asia
Treaty Organization (SEATO). Since India was an advocate
of nonalignment and was opposed to SEATO, conflicting
military strategies, as well as opposing policies toward
China, reduced any impulse that India might otherwise have
had to extend its interests in Southeast Asia. The excesses—
personal, political, and military—of Sukarno in the earlier
years and the military government since have restricted what
might otherwise have been close Indian ties with Indonesia.
The Philippines never has been a country of special interest
to India, and it is even less so now under the dictatorial
regime of President Ferdinand Marcos.

A number of other considerations inhibited closer ties
between India and Southeast Asia: (1) unhappy memories of
past business associations; (2) an antipathy toward Indians
in general, from a cultural point of view; and (3) the
consequences of the Vietnam war.

One can expect more cohesion within the bloc of countries
known as the Association of Southeast Asian Nations
(ASEAN—Thailand, Malaysia, Singapore, Indonesia, and
the Philippines); perhaps within this framework India may
prove to be a cooperating, nonmember country. ASEAN
held its first meeting of heads of government in Bali,
Indonesia, February 23-25, 1976. All indicators point to a
larger role for this regional arrangement in the future.

It is surprising that one must report such moderateness in
India's activities in the Southeast Asian region. Unique
conditions of poverty at home and military complications in

Southeast Asia since the end of the Second World War, plus
the sensitive problem of dealing with the People's Republic
of China, help to explain this near hiatus in India's policy. If
one were to hazard a guess, it may be expected that India ten
years from now will have increased its commercial, cultural,
and diplomatic associations with Southeast Asia greatly: not
as a major partner, and most assuredly not as a dominating
partner, but in modest ways.

East Asia

China

India's policy towards China since 1949 has had three
distinct phases.[19] The first included the early recognition of
the People's Republic of China, the breaking of ties with
Taiwan, and a calculated policy of building close Sino-
Indian friendship. This period is often known as the
"Hindi-Chini Bhai Bhai" era—"India and China are broth-
ers." The government of India encouraged Sino-Indian
friendship associations and supported cultural, trade union,
business, and governmental exchanges of visits between the
two countries; Jawaharlal Nehru at home and India's Ambassador in Peking, K. M. Panikkar, became leading spokesmen for recognition of the People's Republic of China by the
United Nations and all the countries of the world. China's
full absorption of Tibet in 1950-1951, following Chinese
insistence that Tibet remain under the sovereignty of China,
did not end disputes between India and China over other
border territories, however. At least from 1957, on a secret
basis, and from 1959, publicly, the two governments were at
odds over boundary territories involving at least 57,000
square miles, extending from the Aksai Chin area of Ladakh
(in Kashmir), through territories in the northeast of India.
Diplomatic disputation and border provocations that appeared to have come from both sides resulted in the Sino-
Indian border war of 1962. In this war, China easily defeated
the Indian army, and took possession of the lands it claimed.
China had previously occupied sectors in Aksai Chin; it also

retained these territories at the end of the war.[20]

The year 1962 opened the second period of Sino-Indian policy, a period that has been anything but friendly. Diplomatic relations were reduced by calling home ambassadors, and China entered into regular relations with India's other main adversary, Pakistan. India, in turn, altered its strategy by opening special ties with the Soviet Union. This second period continued from 1962 until very recently.[21]

The third period of Sino-Soviet relations is now underway and can be dated from 1976. Diplomatic relations between India and China were restored in 1976, with K. R. Narayana going to Peking as India's ambassador in the late spring of 1976, and with Chen Chao Yuan coming to New Delhi as China's ambassador to India in July 1976. (It is important to note that India announced the ambassadorial exchanges with Pakistan and China not long before the opening of the nonaligned conference in Colombo. It may also may be significant that India took these actions during the period of the Emergency that started on June 26, 1975. Parliamentary debate in India over these conciliatory moves probably would have been more difficult to conclude had the Indian parliament been operating with its full complement in the opposition.)

To date, the latest phase of policies toward China has not resulted in significant trade or cultural exchanges, but they will probably follow. One major complication is that, as success is achieved by India and China in healing the wounds developed over the border controversy, it is to be expected that the USSR will reduce its special attention to India because of the priority it gives to the Sino-Soviet dispute. It will take masterful diplomacy on India's part to remain in balance with both the Soviet Union and China without irritating one or the other or both in the process.

Japan and Korea

Japan has become a major trading partner with India, and this exchange is likely to increase. Japan happens to need raw materials that India wants to export, and India requires many of the manufactured goods that Japan has to market. However, there is no important cultural sense of mutuality between the two, and there is little evidence of any serious effort on the part of Japan or India to develop them. Japanese culture and its approach to modern technology are of interest to Indians, but there is little empathy for Japan and its ways among the leaders of the government of India. Japanese business executives and technical experts have been associated with development projects in India for some years, but the relationships are based on business objectives, and not much more. Nevertheless, businesslike or not, the mutual needs of Japan and India are important enough that the decade ahead will record increasing contact on all levels between the two countries.

As for Korea, both North and South, India has had quite limited relations, except on strictly political or diplomatic levels. India supported the United Nations' resolution condemning the aggression of North Korea against South Korea, and even cooperated in the Korean War with medical and other noncombatant forces. At the end of the Korean War, under UN auspices, General K. S. Thimayya of India and other Indian military personnel assisted in the process of repatriation and helped to bring order in what was a chaotic situation. Since that time, however, India has avoided any major involvement in Korean affairs.

United States of America

The United States is a Pacific power and, because of its economic and military involvement in numerous countries in Asia, has also become a major Asian power, along with the USSR, China, and Japan.[22] The government of India recognizes the special U.S. interests in Asia and the extensive economic aid provided to India since the late 1940s, but India's general policy has been to encourage the reduction of American interests and influences in Asia. The principal reason for this policy has been to soften circumstances that might lead to increased military conflict. India's analysis of both the Korean and the Indochinese wars was that U.S.

intervention created conditions that encouraged Chinese and Soviet support to the communist elements involved, thus opening the possibility of conflict between the major communist countries and the United States, including the potential of nuclear war. Since India considered nuclear war at any point in Asia a potential threat to India itself, opposition to United States' strategic policies was considered to be part of India's search for world peace. India has been more willing to live with the exercise of power from Peking or Moscow in Asia because these major communist states also are Asian states with whom the other peoples of Asia have to live. The United States, on the other hand, is an "outside" Asian power whose actions may raise rather than lower potential levels of conflict. In this same context, the development of Diego Garcia (an island in the Indian Ocean) by the United States as a repair and fueling station for the navy and as a landing, storage, and maintenance point for aircraft is vehemently criticized by India and, indeed, by the other countries that border on the Indian Ocean.

India has not appreciated Washington's strategy (during the Nixon years) of developing better working contacts with Peking, not so much because India opposed some kind of détente between the United States and China, but because India was ignored in the process. It has not been clear to India why the United States would remain uncritical of totalitarian countries, such as China—to say nothing of the closed political systems in a variety of Asian countries, such as South Korea, the Philippines, and Taiwan—and at the same time appear to lack an appreciation for the efforts being made in India to develop its polity and economy under open conditions. During the Emergency (1975-1977), the Indian Government was less vocal in making this argument, but it is likely to return under current Indian political conditions.

USSR

Indo-Soviet accords have been dealt with in a number of

places in this discussion, and there is no need to repeat these points here.[23] The fact is that India and the Soviet Union have been closely related for a number of years, especially after they signed a Treaty of Peace, Friendship and Coopera- tion on August 9, 1971. The Soviet Union has been a good trading partner; much of its trade is carried on under barter arrangements that, while expensive for India in one sense, draw less upon foreign exchange reserves and thus worked to India's benefit. In 1976, Indo-Soviet trade reached one billion dollars. Visits between the heads of state in both countries, as well as other senior officials, are carried on regularly. For example, Mrs. Gandhi made a state visit to Moscow in June 1976, accompanied by her son, Sanjay; this event followed the signing of a new trade agreement in April 1976. The Soviet Foreign Minister, Andrei A. Gromyko, visited India in April 1977 to cement relations with the new government of Morarji Desai. At the end of the discussions, the two governments affirmed the continuation of the 1971 treaty and announced that the USSR was granting a $300 million loan (on favorable terms) to India and that trade between the two countries would be increased by $200 million this year.

In addition to military and trade agreements of impor- tance to India, Soviet advisers in a number of fields have been active in economic planning, agricultural and industrial consultation, and explorations for oil and mineral deposits. Many students from India have attended universities in the the USSR, and a fair number of Soviet scholars have con- ducted research and participated in training in India. On a cultural and social level, there have been meaningful in- creases in understanding between the two countries over the past decade.

India has no desire to reduce its special links with the Soviet Union, but it does wish to be truly nonaligned and to avoid becoming in any way dependent on the Soviet Union—much less a satellite. India's moves to restore better ties with China and with the United States are calculated to reduce its dependency on the Soviet Union.

Conclusions

This review of India's Asian relations reaches the conclusion that, except for the South Asian area itself, India has not chosen to be an Asian power; rather, it has sought ties around the world wherever they happened to be critical for India's interests. It is understandable that a concern for its future ties with China remains a significant part of India's Asia policy, despite the war of 1962 and its aftermath. In this sense, the priority given to Sino-Indian friendship in the Nehru era was only suspended, not ended, by the 1962 war. That Japan is coming into greater focus as part of India's Pacific strategy is easily explained by the economic interests that bind the two countries. Otherwise, most of the issues raised by India relating to Asia have to do with political and military conditions that might, sooner or later, affect India. These matters have arisen during periods of war, as in Korea and Indochina, or they have been reactions to the U.S.-Soviet naval buildups in the Indian Ocean and the Pacific, or at an earlier stage, they have been in criticism of the Southeast Asia Treaty Organization.

Some speculation about the future of India's Asian relations would seem to be in order, however hazardous it is to do so when that part of the world changes so rapidly. First, it may be expected that Sino-Indian ties will improve and that Indo-Soviet relations will decline—at least equally if not more so—over the same period. Second, depending upon the level of domestic tranquility, both within India and in South Asia as a whole, one would expect that all or most of the countries of Southeast Asia—both continental and in the islands—will be increasingly stressed by India. Third, Japan and India are apt to come to agreement, not only on commercial transactions of even greater proportions than at present, but also on cooperative economic and developmental strategies that would be advantageous to the smaller and weaker powers—from Pakistan in the west to Korea in the east. Fourth, India may be expected to continue to work against military buildups by Western, communist, or other countries in the Asian area and to resist overtures for cooperative military arrangements between countries in Asia, or sponsored by one of the major world powers. Fifth, the need for economic assistance in most of the countries in Asia, including India, remains so critical that India will encourage economic cooperation with the United States on a bilateral basis and—with the United States' assistance—through the United Nations and other multilateral organizations. The objective, however, will be to avoid outside political control; and the means will be the establishment of administrative mechanisms among the countries of Asia to manage the funds supplied. Finally, India will continue to recruit and train a major armed force, probably with a nuclear capability, to protect itself in emergencies, even while seeking peaceful solutions by other means.

Much of what has been predicted above for India's future policies in Asia assumes sufficient political stability at home, to say nothing of adequate economic growth, to provide the country with the governmental stability and popular consensus necessary to conduct such an ambitious policy abroad. Regrettably, one cannot be certain that such a combination of favorable factors will exist in India over the next decade. Students of Asia would be well advised to follow India's domestic political economy closely. It will be the critical indicator of India's effectiveness in its future Asian relations.

Notes

1. Published in *Indian Information* (New Delhi: Government of India Information Bureau), October 15, 1946.

2. See Richard L. Park, "India's Foreign Policy," chapter eight in *Foreign Policy in World Politics,* ed. Roy C. Macridis, 5th ed. (Englewood Cliffs, N.J.: Prentice-Hall, 1976), especially the selected bibliography, pp. 337-338. Two recent books that stress policy options in South Asia for the United States are *Southern Asia: The Politics of Poverty and Peace,* Vol. XIII in the "Critical Choices for Americans" series, edited by Donald C. Hellman (Lexington: Lexington

Books, D. C. Heath and Company, 1976), particularly the
essays by Myron Weiner ("Critical Choices for India and
America," pp. 19-78), and John P. Lewis (Growth and
Equity in Two of the Poorest Countries: India and Bangladesh," pp. 79-138); and Lawrence A. Veit, *India's Second
Revolution: The Dimensions of Development* (New York:
McGraw Hill, 1976), Pt. 2, "International Relations and
India's Economy," pp. 101-195. The literature on India's
foreign policy is, of course, vast, including important vol-
umes by Indian authors, officials and nonofficials, many of
which are cited in the books noted above. Of special impor-
tance is Michael Brecher, *India and World Politics: Krishna
Menon's View of the World* (New York: Praeger, 1968).
Norman D. Palmer's *South Asia and United States Policy*
(Boston: Houghton Mifflin, 1966) gives critical attention to
shifts in India's foreign policy and those of other countries
for the period up to 1965. For a broader view, see Wayne
Wilcox, Leo E. Rose, and Gavin Boyd, eds., *Asia and the
International System* (Cambridge, Mass.: Winthrop Pub-
lishers, 1972).

3. A few analyses of the Emergency and its political
implications are Henry C. Hart, ed., *Indira Gandhi's India:
A Political System Reappraised* (Boulder: Westview Press,
1976); Richard L. Park, "Political Crisis in India, 1975,"
Asian Survey 15, no. 11 (November 1975): 996-1013; two
related articles by Rajni Kothari, "The End of an Era" and
"Restoring the Political Process," in *Seminar* (New Delhi)
for January and July 1976; and Marcus F. Franda, *India in an
Emergency,* A Collection of Field Staff Reports (Hanover:
The American Universities Field Staff, 1975).

4. For examples of recent reviews, see Sheldon W. Simon,
"China, the Soviet Union, and the Subcontinental Balance,"
Asian Survey 13, no. 7 (July 1973): 647-658; Robert A.
Scalapino, "The Dragon, the Tiger, and the Wolf: Sino-
Soviet Relations and Their Impact on Asia," *Orbis* 19, no. 3
(Fall 1975): 838-862; and Arthur Jay Klinghoffer, "Sino-
Soviet Relations and the Politics of Oil," *Asian Survey* 16,
no. 6 (June 1976): 540-552. The broader Asian context is

reviewed in Robert A. Scalapino, *Asia and the Road Ahead: Issues for the Major Powers* (Berkeley: University of California Press, 1975); and in Harold C. Hinton, *The Sino-Soviet Confrontation: Implications for the Future* (New York: Crane, Russak and Company, 1976).

5. See Ashok Kapur, "Indo-Soviet Treaty and the Emerging Asian Balance," *Asian Survey* 12, no. 6 (June 1972): 463-474. See also M. R. Masani, "Is India a Soviet Ally?", *Asian Affairs* 1, no. 3 (January-February 1974): 121-135; and Robert H. Donaldson, *Soviet Strategy toward India* (Cambridge, Mass.: Harvard University Press, 1974).

6. K. Subrahmanyam, *The Indian Nuclear Test in Global Perspective* (New Delhi: India International Centre, 1974), outlines India's policy on nuclear power. For a critical analysis see David Van Praagh, "India's Bomb," *Asian Affairs* 1, no. 6 (July-August 1974): 357-370. See also James E. Dougherty, "Nuclear Proliferation in Asia," *Orbis* 19, no. 3 (Fall 1975): 925-957; and S. P. Seth, "India's Atomic Profile," *Pacific Community* 6, no. 2 (January 1975): 272-282.

7. See the table on p. 131.

8. The details are given in *India News* 15, no. 39, of December 24, 1976 (Washington, D.C.: Information Service, Embassy of India), p. 3.

9. See Norman D. Palmer, "India in 1976: The Politics of Depoliticization," *Asian Survey* 17, no. 2 (February 1977): 175.

10. For background, see Richard S. Newell, *The Politics of Afghanistan* (Ithaca: Cornell University Press, 1972), especially pp. 186-194.

11. Palmer, "India in 1976," p. 176.

12. See Anwar H. Syed, "Pakistan in 1976: Business as Usual," *Asian Survey* 17, no. 2 (February 1977): 187-190. See also Lawrence Ziring, "Recent Trends in Pakistan's Foreign Policy," *Asian Affairs* 2, no. 5 (May/June 1975): 295-307; Zalmay Khalilzad, "Pakistan: The Making of a Nuclear Power," *Asian Survey* 16, no. 6 (June 1976): 580-592; and G. W. Choudhury, "Reflections on Sino-Pakistan Relations," *Pacific Community* 7, no. 2 (January 1976): 248-270.

13. *New York Times,* March 13, 1977, p. 5.

14. Syed, "Pakistan in 1976, p. 188. The protocol signed on May 19, 1977, in Islamabad by Iran and Pakistan outlined a series of projects for the expansion of mutual trade between the two countries.

15. One recent thorough review is Talukder Maniruzzaman, "Bangladesh in 1976: Struggle for Survival as an Independent State," *Asian Survey* 17, no. 2 (February 1977): 191-200.

16. See Prakash C. Lohani, "Nepal 1975: Not a Normal Year," *Asian Survey* 16, no. 2 (February 1976): 140-145; also T. K. Jayaraman and O. L. Shrestha, "Some Trade Problems of Landlocked Nepal,"*Asian Survey* 16, no. 12 (December 1976): 1113-1123. For Bhutan, see Leo E. Rose, *The Politics of Bhutan* (Ithaca: Cornell University Press, 1977).

17. See Robert N. Kearney, *The Politics of Ceylon (Sri Lanka)* (Ithaca: Cornell University Press, 1973). Also useful are George J. Lerski, "Sri Lanka Turns East," *Asian Affairs,* 1, no. 3 (January-February 1974): 184-196; and P. V. J. Jayasekera, "Sri Lanka in 1976: Changing Strategies and Confrontation," *Asian Survey* 17, no. 2 (February 1977): 208-217.

18. A few relevant references are David Wurfel, "Southeast Asian Alignments," *International Journal* 29, no. 3 (Summer 1974): 441-477; Shiro Inoue, "New Aspects of Economic Cooperation in Asia," *Pacific Community* 7, no. 1 (October 1975): 78-91; and "A Survey of Asia in 1976: Part 2," *Asian Survey* 17, no. 2 (February 1977), especially the articles by R. William Liddle (Indonesia) and Lela Noble (Philippines). For an early Indian appraisal, see K. M. Panikar, *The Future of South-East Asia: An Indian View* (New York: Macmillan, 1943).

19. For East Asia, see the references in note 4. See also Zillur R. Khan, "Japanese Relations with India, Pakistan, and Bangladesh," *Pacific Affairs* 48, no. 4 (Winter 1975-76): 541-557.

20. For provocative reviews of the Sino-Indian Border war, see Neville Maxwell, *India's China War* (London:

Jonathan Cape, 1970); and Allen S. Whiting, *The Chinese Calculus of Deterrence: India and Indochina* (Ann Arbor: University of Michigan Press, 1975).

21. See Mohammad Habib Sidky, "Chinese World Strategy and South Asia: The China Factor in Indo-Pakistani Relations," *Asian Survey* 16, no. 10 (October 1976): 965-980.

22. See the references in note 2. See also "United States–South Asian Relations in the 1970's: A Conference Report," *Orbis* 17, no. 4 (Winter 1974): 1383-1395; "Reflections on U.S. Interests in Asia, 1975-1980," by the editors of *Orbis* 19, no. 3 (Fall 1975); and S. P. Seth, "The Indian Ocean and Indo-American Relations," *Asian Survey* 15, no. 8 (August 1975): 645-655.

23. See Kapur, "Indo-Soviet Treaty." See also Robert H. Donaldson, "India: The Soviet Stake in Stability," *Asian Survey* 12, no. 6 (June 1972): 475-492; R. V. R. Chandrasekhara Rao, "Indo-Soviet Economic Relations," *Asian Survey* 13, no. 8 (August 1973): 793-801; and Harold C. Hinton, "The Soviet Campaign for Collective Security in Asia," *Pacific Community* 7, no. 2 (January 1976): 147-161.

8. Asian Actors and Issues

Morton I. Abramowitz

The very useful chapters in this volume provide a picture of the Asian scene as Americans perceive it to be seen by the different actors of the region. In this respect, the chapters are a scholarly version of Rashomon and may result in looking through a glass darkly. However, this does not detract from the overall value of this approach.

The various chapters deal with the perceptions held by two actors, the People's Republic of China and Japan, and the perceptions of a collective set of actors known as Southeast Asia. In addition, Mr. Scalapino's chapter deals with all of the regional actors in a broad fashion. However, some less towering, but very important, actors get short shrift, notably North and South Korea.

I will begin by adding my comments on the perceptions of these actors to the comments made by the other authors. In addition, from this welter of differing national perceptions, I will draw some generalizations about the Asian scene that seem to me to be the major topics or issues inherent to the international relations of the region.

This paper does not necessarily represent the views of either the Department of Defense or the United States government. What follows are some purely personal thoughts. I want to thank Middleton Martin, David Lohmann, and Ken Richeson for their assistance.

I am sure that my comments and approach are affected by my own bias—a government bias that tends to make me concentrate on defining the questions and issues in terms of national security and in ways that would affect public policy and policy-makers.

The Actors

China

In discussing contempory China, modesty should be very much in order, although it rarely is. Both within and outside the U.S. government, our capacity to understand China's political processes has been shown to be limited at best. It is only necessary to cite the Cultural Revolution or the reemergence and subsequent fall of Teng Hsiao-p'ing. Our ability to chart Chinese policy in advance may now be no better than in the past.

With this in mind I would like to take issue with Professor Barnett's conclusion that Chinese perceptions of their vulnerability vis-á-vis the Soviet Union will be the paramount factor shaping the PRC's foreign policy and that there will therefore be little significant reorientation in China's foreign policy for the foreseeable future. National security is an abiding concern of most powers, and I agree that security perceptions will play an important role in shaping Chinese policy. However, I am reluctant to concur in the view that this factor is more significant than a host of other factors. In particular, I would stress the importance of domestic politics, a factor that Professor Barnett discusses but subordinates to Chinese security interests.

If Professor Barnett is correct, we should not expect the PRC's policies toward the USSR and the West to be the subject of internal PRC debates. However, relations with the Soviet Union have been a part of almost every major Chinese leadership debate. In addition, the policy of technology imports from the West has been repeatedly questioned during the most recent campaigns. Finally if the threat posed by the Soviet Union were the major determinant of Chinese policy, certainly it would be equally rational for the Chinese to recognize their military inferiority and seek a more accommodating relationship with the USSR, if only to improve the military equation. Given this rationale, and based on my own experience, I would elevate domestic politics to near-paramount importance as a determinant of Chinese policy, foreign and domestic.

I do not want to overemphasize this one point, for there are obviously many factors affecting Chinese perceptions of their external problems. What is important, however, is that we should be wary of defining the issues in narrow terms that may facilitate prediction but not necessarily comprehension. I am concerned, for example, that a security-oriented analysis of the influences operating on Chinese policy decisions may lead to sanguine estimates of the durability of the Sino-Soviet split. I recognize that there are good reasons for believing that the split will be perpetuated. However, by concentrating on the reasons for continuity, we may be ignoring the possibilities for change, in part, perhaps, because of the difficulties of dealing with the profound consequences of change in Sino-Soviet relations for the international politics of the region.

Soviet Union

I agree with Mr. Scalapino's assessment that the containment of China has been the principal motivation for extension of Soviet military and political influence in Asia. However, for some reason the perception of the Soviet Union in Asia is driven more by fears of possible action than by an analysis of Soviet capabilities. In other words, there is a tendency to ascribe to the Soviet Union a role and capabilities that approximate the perception of their intentions but that are not consistent with their actual current capabilities. Specifically, despite their buildup of land and air forces along the Sino-Soviet border since 1965 and their continued improvement of their Pacific fleet, conventional Soviet military capabilities in Asia are still limited. In fact, although Soviet military forces along the Sino-Soviet border

exceed those required to defend against any attack the
Chinese might launch, Soviet conventional offensive options vis-á-vis the Chinese are extremely limited and might
not be decisive in any major conflict. This practical limit on
the Soviet ability to project military power throughout Asia
currently sets limits to the Soviet capability to exercise
expanded political influence in the area, even if that is their
intent.

Obviously, this capability may change over time. Moreover, there are ways other than military ways to project
influence, and a case can be made for describing the Soviets
as an imperial power. However, Soviet actions in Asia
evidence no burning design for regional or subregional
hegemony. Instead, Soviet actions appear to be driven by a
desire to counter Chinese influence in whatever arena it
appears and, to a lesser extent, to eliminate U.S. influence in
the region. This distinction between seeking hegemony and
countering PRC and U.S. influence is not lost on the other
nations of the region and also limits Soviet actions in Asia.
For example, the Soviets will undoubtedly seek to expand
diplomatic and economic relations within the area and are
probably willing to do such things as resume aid programs,
say in Indonesia. However, unless there are significant increases in either Chinese or U.S. influence in the area, it is
unlikely that the Soviets will go much further than this.
Therefore, given the perception that the Soviet programs in
Asia are designed to counter PRC and, second, U.S. influence, the impact of these efforts will be measured primarily
in terms of the Sino-Soviet dispute and in Japanese perceptions of the overall Soviet-American military balance.

However, I should note that all of the key Asian actors are
becoming increasingly concerned about the buildup of
Soviet naval power in the Pacific. Although the Soviet
Pacific Fleet has historically received less emphasis than
have the other Soviet fleets, it has been systematically improved, both quantitatively and qualitatively, in recent
years. If this trend continues, the Soviet ability to threaten
the lines of communications of these key actors may at some

time in the future be matched by a Soviet propensity to do so.

Japan

Japan, like China, challenges our predictive capabilities. On the one hand, since Japan is an open society, it is easier to isolate and weigh the factors affecting Japan's perceptions and actions in the foreign policy sphere than it is for China, which is a closed society. On the other hand, Japan is much more vulnerable than China to the impact of external events such as the global recession and the oil embargo. Although Japan has demonstrated remarkable creativity and adaptiveness in response to these events, in the final analysis, its economy, and hence its social and political well-being, continue to be dependent on events far beyond Japan's control. Similarly, given the current capabilities of its self-defense forces, Japan's security and way of life depend to some extent on circumstances not within Japan's own control, notably the American perception that Japan is of vital importance to U.S. security—a perception held by all U.S. policy-makers and one not likely to change.

And yet, given Japan's vulnerability to external events, it is difficult to foresee (as Mr. Hellmann's chapter illustrates) whether Japan will continue to be satisfied with its current, self-consciously assumed role of economic giant and limited military power. A Japanese decision to abandon this role would necessarily be influenced by many factors. One such factor is whether the world will permit the Japanese to pursue policies essential to their economic vitality in the absence of significant Japanese military power and political leverage. Another factor will be the Japanese people's present antipathy to the use of force as an instrument of national policy. In this regard it should be remembered that ostensibly ingrained national attitudes can change quickly—witness the rapid change in the Japanese people's attitude toward armed conflict, a change from the glorification of war in the 1930s to revulsion of conflict in the immediate post–World War II period. A third major factor affecting any significant increase in Japanese military capabilities is their perception of the threats posed to Japan and the U.S. capabilities to deter and, if necessary, counter these threats. The absence of overt threats to Japan suggests that sentiments for rearmament will remain within bounds for the foreseeable future. However, indicators of American unwillingness or inability to play an important role in the Western Pacific could create sufficient Japanese concern to energize a Japanese rearmament effort. This is why ensuring that Japanese perceptions of the U.S. role in Asia remain positive has been a central feature of U.S. foreign and defense policy.

North and South Korea

I regret the lack of attention that the other authors paid to the two Koreas. These two actors are increasingly important in Asian international politics because of their growing national strength, their significant capacity for independent military action, and their increasing independence from presumed great-power patrons.

Given the depth of their enmity, it is interesting that both Koreas appear to perceive themselves, each other, and the forces at work outside the Korean peninsula in much the same manner and have responded with remarkably similar courses of action. Specifically, developments in U.S.-PRC and U.S.-USSR relations since 1972 have heightened the uncertainty of both North and South about their relations with their great-power sponsors. As a result of this uncertainty, the two Koreas have hastened their quests for greater flexibility and self-reliance in the political, economic, and military spheres—what Mr. Scalapino calls the trend away from the politics of alliance toward the policies of equidistance—with a strong dose of pragmatism as a result. On both sides, this quest has taken the form of increased military budgets, independent diplomatic initiatives, parallel efforts to improve domestic weapon production capabilities and to diversify sources of arms supply, and, in the case of North Korea, skilled use of the leverage offered by Sino-Soviet differences.

Lest I overemphasize these similarities between the two

Koreas, it should be noted that each actor has some special characteristics that also influence the perceptions of the other actors in the region. There is a widely held perception that the North Koreans are irrational and that Kim Il Sung is committed to unifying Korea either under his leadership or on his own terms during his lifetime. However, time is running out, and South Korea grows steadily stronger, economically and militarily. In the South, President Park Chung Hee's government is frequently perceived to be overly authoritarian and vulnerable to domestic unrest. This perception has led to concern over the future stability of South Korea and to questioning by members of Congress and the U.S. public of the U.S. role in Korea. The net result is a perception of Korea as a tinderbox, waiting only for a spark that could result in open conflict at any time.

The risk of renewed hostilities on the peninsula is mitigated by the substantial parity of opposing forces, the presence of U.S. forces, and by the countervailing pressures from allies against high-risk policies. But the fears, animosities, proximity of contending forces, high state of military preparedness, and policy independence on both sides create a climate for conflict whose prevention may be beyond the control of the great powers.

Southeast Asia

It is, of course, difficult to treat Southeast Asia as a collective actor, and both Pauker and Scalapino deal comprehensively with the heterogeneity and attendant conflicts and the tendency toward fragmentation in Southeast Asia. However, I do not quite agree with Pauker that there is less direct interest and attention by the major powers in Southeast Asia than at any time in recent history. Both Soviet and Chinese interests are high, since Southeast Asia remains an area of Sino-Soviet competition. There is less U.S. attention, but it should be noted that the level of our earlier interest was mostly a function of our concern with Vietnam. Elsewhere in the region—in the Philippines, Thailand, Singapore, Malaysia, and Indonesia—our interests have remained. It is perhaps better to say that the military involvement of the major powers has diminished. The political interests have remained, and the economic ones have certainly grown.

As an important subregional actor, similar to the Koreas in Northeast Asia, only Vietnam possesses the actual or potential capacity to influence the international politics of Asia as a whole. For the moment it appears that Vietnam will concentrate on consolidating its political power and developing its economy. In the international area, it seems intent on improving its state-to-state relations. However, these are only initial perceptions of what Vietnam may do, based on what they say. What will be more important is what they do. Should their rhetoric change, it will still be necessary to differentiate between revolutionary rhetoric and interventionist intent. In either case, the complexity and breadth of the internal political and economic problems confronting Vietnam may be such as to inhibit serious national effort, other than rhetorical, to realize and exercise their potential to affect external events.

The Issues

Let me now turn to what I believe are some of the major issues or considerations relating to their Asian policies that must be faced by the policy-makers of each country.

In considering these issues, it is important to remember that the Asian environment is clearly different from the European one. In Europe there has long been what might be called a line—a line that separated the communist countries from the noncommunist countries and that influenced and limited the interactions between these countries. Given the advent of possible communist participation in Western European governments, that line may be dimming. However, there has been a line, and both East and West have known it. In Asia the stage is not so clearly marked, and the room for country interaction appears much wider. Throughout Asia we have already seen such diverse changes in relationships that generalization becomes difficult. Yet there are common issues and trends that policy-makers must come to grips with.

Sino-Soviet Relations

The most significant and pervasive issue that must be addressed by each country, certainly in the short run, is the Sino-Soviet relationship. The impact of their differences, of course, has been pervasive both in Europe and in Asia. It has changed the capabilities of China vis-à-vis the rest of the countries of Asia, and it has changed the perceptions of the Asian countries about the nature of their dealings with those two countries. No other development has contributed more to the psychological well-being of Asia, and no other element has been more important in permitting what Scalapino calls the politics of equidistance. Conversely, any change in the situation would have tremendous impact in Asia and, of course, the world, depending upon the nature of that change.

Each country in the area must, therefore, take full cognizance of the character of these tensions, even if they choose not to articulate their thoughts about them. They must weigh their durability. They must consider the implications of a reduction of Sino-Soviet tensions or a limited rapprochement. All countries, but particularly the larger countries such as Japan, must determine whether it is in their capability, either individually or in conjunction with other countries, to affect in any way the course of Sino-Soviet relations. As for the less powerful, these countries must be able to handle Sino-Soviet competition in their own backyards should it significantly increase.

Interdependence vs. National Assertiveness

The second key issue facing the policy-makers of each country is the resolution of the apparently conflicting trends of regional and global interdependence and growing national assertiveness and independence. The weakening of the bipolar environment has contributed significantly to the increased independence of the regional actors. As a result, great-power influence in Asia is less than at any time since World War II. At the same time there has been an increasing interdependence in economics and technology—an interdependence that is essential to both the economic development and the growth of the military capabilities of the Asian nations.

These conflicting trends of independence and interdependence have had a mixed impact on Asia. The major powers, the more affluent countries, have had to reevaluate their interests in the less-developed world. No longer are international relations a zero-sum game in which influence must be preserved at all costs. Now the major powers can even welcome increased independence in the Third World, relying on the bonds of interdependence to act at least as a minimal constraint. On the other hand, the developing countries must come to grips with a more complicated notion of policy. In addition, these different forces must be reconciled by the developing countries. If not, the drive for independence may prejudice chances for mutually beneficial arrangements among regional neighbors. ASEAN is a case in point, since its future is particularly dependent on the successful resolution of the conflicting forces of independence and interdependence.

The drive for independence and the associated growth of national assertiveness can also have profound effects on regional peace and stability. We have already noted the case of Korea and the attendant risks of conflict resulting from the increased independence from great-power constraints. Elsewhere it is possible that military forces, as symbols of national power or for domestic political purposes, will be increased despite the absence of real threats. The result could be destabilizing as threats are perceived where none are intended and arms races begin. Equally unsettling might be for a host country to decide that the existence of foreign bases on its soil is incompatible with its nationalistic aims. Any resultant withdrawals of military forces could have profound effects on the balance of military power in the region.

Finally, it is possible that some actors could again, in the name of nationalism, advocate adventurism with a destabilizing result.

Let me reiterate, I am neither predicting nor prescribing—I am simply stating the possible. I believe that the potential for regional instability inherent in national assertiveness warrants the most serious consideration by the policymakers in all countries.

Economics

The third and probably the most comprehensive issue that has to be addressed by all actors is the role of economic considerations in the determination of policy and in the future politics of the region. Economic issues—finance, trade, foreign investment—cannot but have a major impact on the foreign policies of Japan, Korea, and a whole host of developed countries. In China the question is put normally in terms of how much reliance should be placed on outside technology.

These issues are probably not in themselves destabilizing. However, there are other economic issues that could possibly result in conflict in the area, such as conflicting claims of offshore drilling rights, the delineation of economic zones, and disputes over fishing rights. Precedents already exist in the Paracels and disputes over the Spratlys. Budding arguments here and elsewhere involve virtually every country in the area and contain considerable potential for regional instability—instability that could lead to major-power involvement. Resource constraints and increasing industrialization of the Asian area point to the increasing importance of these disputed territories. In short, economics can foster conflict as well as cooperation, and the way each country perceives its economic problems and comes to grips with them will affect stability in the area. Here domestic politics may well be paramount.

The nations in Asia will also need to assess their own potential for economic growth, contend with highly divergent growth rates in the region, and develop policies that deal effectively with rising expectations that may exceed their economic development and capabilities. This last issue is especially important, for its brings with it the possibility of internal political instability. Finally each country in the region will also have to come to some understanding with the major powers of the world in order to achieve any semblance of viable economic growth.

Each nation will also have to decide whether and in what ways economic power can be employed as an instrument of foreign policy in the region. The possible resolutions to these questions will in all likelihood vary considerably by actor. For example, Japan may find at some point that its limited military capabilities can no longer be substituted for by economic power as an instrument of foreign policy. On the other hand, Vietnam may find itself seriously deficient in economic leverage.

Internal Conflict

Lastly, I think each actor, with the possible exception of Japan, must face the possibility of internal conflict. Here I do not mean the vagaries of internal politics, although they may be instrumental in stimulating internal conflict. Rather I mean the instability that is associated with armed conflict and that more immediately affects the relationships among nations.

For the present we have the armed insurgencies in Southeast Asia—Thailand, Malaysia, Indonesia, and the Philippines. These insurgencies can take on broader significance if the insurgents receive assistance from an outside source. Should this occur, they can assume regional or even global importance as different nations evaluate the effect of internal conflict on regional power balances as well as other balances. I am not necessarily referring to the past—to the American experience in Vietnam—although the parallels clearly exist. Rather I am discussing current and future possibilities. A case in point: Singapore and Indonesia are more concerned about insurgent activities in Thailand and Malaysia than the Japanese, but the Japanese will keep their eyes on how the United States (and the PRC and Soviet Union) reacts to the Thai and Malaysian situations.

Aside from the perceptions of all nations towards countries experiencing internal conflict, such conflict can have a direct destabilizing impact. For example, internal conflict could cause the affected country either to withdraw from or to seek commitments or agreements with other nations, which could affect power relations in the area. Recent U.S.-Thai developments may be a case in point. In addition, domestic strife in one country can only make neighboring countries more reticent in their dealings with the affected country and with one another. Stated another way, internal conflict may raise barriers to cooperation simply by creating a climate of uncertainty. Each actor must assess the significance of internal threats to regional stability and must determine which methods are reasonable for dealing with the internal conflict of another country.

In this short review, I have made some comments on how the actors in Asia may perceive their regional environment and how this perception might influence their interactions. Admittedly this is a difficult task at best and should be approached with caution.

The policy formulation process in other nations is no doubt different from our own; however, I suspect that it is often no less diffuse and involved. Therefore the identification of paramount factors influencing the perceptions and actions of others is fraught with danger. This is especially true in the case of China, where domestic political debates may well be as important in determining future Chinese foreign policy as will be the continued presence of Soviet forces on China's borders. Japan, like China, challenges our predictive power, and we must continually be aware of the fact that Japan's perceptions and policies are shaped to a large extent by external events. In addition, when dealing with the Soviet Union and with the perceptions it creates in the minds of others, we must be careful to separate form from substance. In other words, we should not ascribe to the Soviet

Union a role and capability that approximates our perception of their intentions and that does not reflect their true capabilities in Asia in general, not just along the Sino-Soviet border. Finally, no discussion of Asia and Asians can exclude Korea. The possibility of renewed hostilities in a highly volatile environment will have an important impact on perceptions and policies throughout the region for the foreseeable future.

In addition to a discussion of perceptions, I have described some of the key issues to be addressed by all Asian nations: Sino-Soviet relations, the problems of interdependence vs. national assertiveness, various economic issues, and the possibility of internal conflict. These issues are serious ones whose resolution will profoundly influence the peace and stability of the region. The gravity of the questions, however, is not meant to imply undue pessimism on their future resolution. My own belief is that the encouraging factors—the passive mood of the major powers toward the area, the exceptional rates of economic growth in Asia, the too-often-disparaged efforts at regional cooperation, and the quality of the leadership as compared to other less-developed areas—will strongly influence the ways these key issues are dealt with.

Selected Bibliography

China

Barnett, A. Doak. *China Policy*. Washington: The Brookings Institution, 1977.

Chiu, Hungdah. *China and the Question of Taiwan: Documents and Analysis*. New York: Praeger, 1973.

Clubb, Oliver Edmund. *China and Russia: The "Great Game."* New York: Columbia University Press, 1971.

Cohen, Jerome Alan, and Chiu, Hungdah. *People's China and International Law: A Documentary Study*. Princeton: Princeton University Press, 1974.

Cooper, Franklin John. *China's Foreign Aid*. Lexington, Mass.: Heath Lexington Books, 1976.

Fairbank, John K. *China Perceived*. New York: Knopf, 1974.

Gittings, John. *The World and China*. New York: Harper and Row, 1974.

Hellmann, Donald C., ed. *China and Japan: A New Balance of Power*. Lexington, Mass.: Lexington Books, 1976.

Hsiao, Gene T., ed. *Sino-American Detente and Its Policy Implications*. New York: Praeger, 1974.

Hsiung, James Chieh. *Law and Policy in China's Foreign Relations*. New York: Columbia University Press, 1972.

Mueller, Peter G., and Ross, Douglas A. *China and Japan— Emerging Global Powers*. New York: Praeger, 1975.

Ojha, Ishwer C. *Chinese Foreign Policy in An Age of Transition.* 2d ed. Boston: Beacon Press, 1971.

Scalapino, Robert A. *Asia and the Road Ahead.* Berkeley: University of California Press, 1975.

Syed, Anwar H. *China and Pakistan.* Amherst: University of Massachusetts Press, 1974.

Taylor, Jay. *China and Southeast Asia: Peking's Relations with Revolutionary Movements.* Expanded ed. New York: Praeger, 1976.

Weng, Byron S. *Peking's UN Policy: Continuity and Change.* New York: Praeger, 1972.

Whiting, Allen S. *The Chinese Calculus of Deterrence: India and Indochina.* Ann Arbor: University of Michigan Press, 1975.

Wilcox, F. O., ed. *China and the Great Powers: Relations with the United States, the Soviet Union and Japan.* New York: Praeger, 1974.

Zagoria, Donald S. *The Sino-Soviet Conflict, 1956-1961.* Princeton: Princeton University Press, 1962

Japan

Brzezinski, Zbigniew. *The Fragile Blossom.* New York: Harper and Row, 1972.

Clapp, Priscilla, and Halperin, Morton H., eds. *United States–Japanese Relations: The 1970s.* Cambridge, Mass.: Harvard University Press, 1974.

Clough, Ralph N. *East Asia and U.S. Security.* Washington: The Brookings Institution, 1975.

Curtis, Gerald L., ed. *Japanese-American Relations in the 1970s.* Washington: American Assembly, 1970.

Destler, I. M., et al. *Managing an Alliance: The Politics of U.S.-Japanese Relations.* Washington: The Brookings Institution, 1976.

Emerson, John K. *Arms, Yen and Power: The Japanese Dilemma.* New York: Dunellen, 1971.

Hellmann, Donald C. *Japan and East Asia: The New International Order.* New York: Praeger, 1972.

Langdon, Frank. *Japan's Foreign Policy,* Berkeley: University of California Press, 1973.

Lee, Chaejin. *Japan Faces China.* Baltimore: Johns Hopkins, 1976.

Morley, James William, ed. *Forecast for Japan: Security in the 1970s.* Princeton: Princeton University Press, 1972.

Patrick, Hugh, and Rosovsky, Henry, eds. *Asia's New Giant: How the Japanese Economy Works.* Washington: The Brookings Institution, 1976.

Scalapino, Robert A. *American-Japanese Relations in a Changing Era.* New York: Library Press, 1972.

————, ed. *The Foreign Policy of Modern Japan.* Berkeley: University of California Press, forthcoming.

Weinstein, Martin E. *Japan's Postwar Defense Policy, 1947-1968.* New York: Columbia University Press, 1971.

South Asia

Ayoob, Mohammed. *India, Pakistan and Bangladesh: Search for a New Relationship.* New Delhi: Indian Council of World Affairs, 1974.

Barnds, William J. *India, Pakistan and the Great Powers.* New York: Praeger, 1972.

Brown, W. Norman. *The United States and India, Pakistan and Bangladesh.* 3rd ed. Cambridge, Mass.: Harvard University Press, 1972.

Burke, S. M. *Mainsprings of Indian and Pakistani Foreign Policies.* Minneapolis: University of Minnesota Press, 1974.

Datar, Asha. *India's Economic Relations with the USSR and Eastern Europe, 1953-1969.* Cambridge: Cambridge University Press, 1972.

Maxwell, Neville. *India's China War.* London: Jonathan Cape, 1970.

Mehta, Balraj. *India and the World Oil Crisis.* New Delhi: Verry Publishers, 1974.

Misra, K. P. *The Role of the United Nations in the Indo-Pakistani Conflict, 1971.* Delhi: Vikas, 1973.

Nanda, B. R., ed. *Indian Foreign Policy: The Nehru Years.* Honolulu: University of Hawaii Press, 1976.

Rana, A. P. *The Imperatives of Nonalignment: A Conceptual Study of India's Foreign Policy Strategy in the Nehru Period.* Delhi: Macmillan of India, 1976.

Rushbrook-Williams, L. *The East Pakistan Tragedy.* London: Stacey, 1972.

Sen Gupta, Bhabani. *Communism in Indian Politics.* New York: Columbia University Press, 1972.

——. *The Fulcrum of Asia:Relations among China, India, Pakistan and the USSR.* New York: Pegasus, 1970.

Subrahmanyam, K. *The Indian Nuclear Test in a Global Perspective.* New Delhi: India International Center, 1974.

Wilcox, Wayne. *The Emergence of Bangladesh: Problems and Opportunities for a Redefined American Policy in South Asia.* Washington: American Enterprise Institute for Public Policy Research, 1973.

Southeast Asia

Agung, Ide Anak Agung Gde. *Twenty Years of Indonesian Foreign Policy, 1945-1965.* The Hague: Mouton, 1973.

Allen, Richard. *A Short Introduction to the History and Politics of Southeast Asia.* New York: Oxford University Press, 1970.

Butwell, Richard. *Southeast Asia: A Political Introduction.* New York: Praeger, 1975.

Cady, John F. *The United States and Burma.* Cambridge, Mass.: Harvard University Press, 1976.

Chawla, Sudershan; Gurtov, Melvin; and Marsot, Alain-Gerard, eds. *Southeast Asia under the New Balance of Power.* New York: Praeger, 1974.

Dake, C. A. *In the Spirit of the Red Banteng: Indonesian Communists Between Moscow and Peking.* The Hague: Mouton, 1973.

Hellmann, Donald C., ed. *Southern Asia: The Politics of Poverty and Peace.* Lexington, Mass.: Lexington Books, 1976.

Manglapus, Raul S. *Japan in Southeast Asia.* Washington: Carnegie Endowment for International Peace, 1976.

Mehden, Fred R. von der. *South-East Asia, 1930-1970: The*

Legacy of Colonialism and Nationalism. New York: Norton, 1974.

Pool, Peter A. *The United States and Indochina: From FDR to Nixon.* Hinsdale, Ill.: Dryden Press, 1973.

Simon, Sheldon W. *War and Politics in Cambodia.* Durham, N.C.: Duke University Press, 1974.

Weinstein, Franklin B. *Indonesian Foreign Policy and the Dilemma of Dependence: From Sukarno to Soeharto.* Ithaca, N.Y.: Cornell University Press, 1976.

Soviet Union

Aspaturian, Vernon V. *Process and Power in Soviet Foreign Policy.* Boston: Little, Brown and Co., 1971.

Donaldson, Robert O. *Soviet Policy Toward India: Ideology and Strategy.* Cambridge, Mass.: Harvard University Press, 1974.

Jacobsen, C. G. *Soviet Strategy—Soviet Foreign Policy: Military Considerations Affecting Soviet Policy-Making.* Glasgow: MacLehose—The University Press, 1972.

Jukes, Geoffrey. *The Soviet Union in Asia.* Berkeley: University of California Press, 1973.

Kanet, Roger E., ed. *The Soviet Union and the Developing Nations.* Baltimore: The Johns Hopkins University Press, 1974.

————, and Bahry, Donna, eds. *Soviet Economic and Political Relations with the Developing World.* New York: Praeger, 1975.

Kohler, Foy D., et al. *Soviet Strategy for the Seventies: From Cold War to Peaceful Coexistence.* Coral Gables, Fla.: Center for Advanced International Studies, University of Miami, 1973.

Kulski, W. W. *The Soviet Union in World Affairs: A Documented Analysis, 1964-1972.* Syracuse, N.Y.: Syracuse University Press, 1973.

London, Kurt, ed. *The Soviet Impact on World Politics.* New York: Hawthorn, 1974.

McLane, Charles B. *Soviet-Asian Relations.* New York: Columbia University Press, 1973.

Sen Gupta, Bhabani. *Soviet-Asian Relations in the 1970s and Beyond*. New York: Praeger, 1976.

Ulam, Adam B. *Expansion and Coexistence: Soviet Foreign Policy, 1917-1973*. 2d ed. New York: Praeger, 1974.

Vucinich, Wayne S., ed. *Russian and Asia: Essays on the Influence of Russia on the Asian Peoples*. Stanford, Calif.: Hoover Institution, 1972.

Wesson, Robert G. *The Russian Dilemma: A Political and Geopolitical View*. Brunswick: Rutgers University Press, 1974.